HENRY MOORE AT THE SERPENTINE

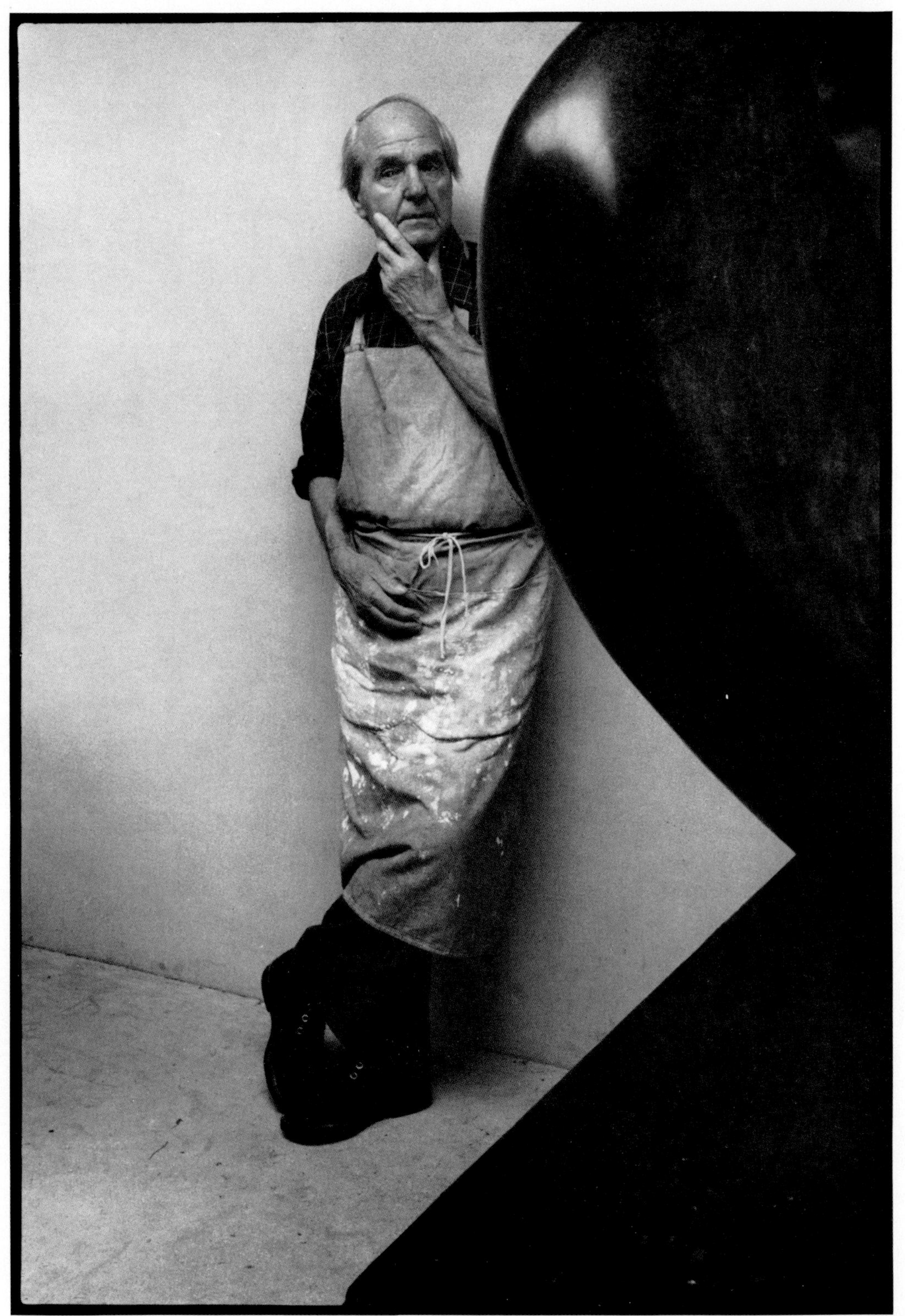

HENRY MOORE
AT THE SERPENTINE

80th birthday exhibition of recent carvings and bronzes
Serpentine Gallery and Kensington Gardens
1 July – 8 October 1978

An Arts Council exhibition

PREFACE

Henry Moore has often asserted that sculpture 'is an art of the open air' and his monumental works can be seen out of doors in most of the world's great cities. Nevertheless, he has never had a predominantly open-air exhibition in London. There could therefore be no more appropriate way to celebrate his eightieth birthday (on 30 July) than to display ten of his large bronzes in one of the most beautiful of London's parks. Most of these works, and many of the fourteen stone and wood carvings shown inside the gallery, have been made in the last decade.

The exhibition has been directed by David Sylvester and Susan Grayson. The artist himself has given much invaluable advice on the placing of the outdoor pieces. David Mitchinson, archivist to The Henry Moore Foundation, has assisted in making the selection of maquettes and natural objects from the studio.

The Arts Council also wishes to thank the following:
The Department of the Environment, in particular Lady Birk, the Under-Secretary of State, for making Kensington Gardens available; Mr James Ellis, Directing Architect, Directorate of Ancient Monuments and Historic Buildings, for arranging the preparation of the sculpture sites; Mrs Betty Tinsley, the artist's secretary, for untiring practical help; Frank and John Farnham, for painstaking help with packing and transport; Michel Muller and Malcolm Woodward, for supervising the installation of the outdoor sculptures; Mary Moore, for the loan of some carvings; The Henry Moore Foundation for the loan of other works, including new bronze casts of several outdoor pieces; Mrs Irina Moore, for her encouragement and support.

Joanna Drew
Director of Art

Frontispiece: Photograph of Henry Moore taken in 1977 by Arnold Newman for an exhibition opening at the National Portrait Gallery in spring 1979, arranged in association with *The Sunday Times*

In almost all cases the photographs are the artist's own except
Plates 7, 12   Errol Jackson
Plates A, 1, 17   Gemma Levine
Plates 8, 9   Reinhard Friedrich

ISBN 0 7287 0177 4
Catalogue designed by Roger Huggett/Sinc
Printed in England by Raithby, Lawrence & Company Ltd, Leicester and London

INTRODUCTION by David Sylvester

This exhibition consists mainly of sculptures made since the Henry Moore retrospective at the Tate in 1968. It also includes a few slightly earlier pieces that seem especially relevant. While the exhibition coincides with the artist's eightieth birthday, it is not a pious gesture but the fulfilment of a genuine need: only incidentally is it a tribute; it is primarily a report. The work Moore has done in the last ten years has been almost unseen in Britain. We normally keep abreast of an artist's production by seeing his work in one-man shows in commercial galleries, but with Moore this has come to be impossible since so much of his major work is now on a very large scale and meant to be placed out of doors. Because the present show is mounted both within the Serpentine Gallery and in the surrounding park, it is able to present a representative selection of the sculpture Moore has been doing in recent years in every sort of size and material.

There is also a wide variety, as we have come to expect of any batch of work by Moore, in terms of sculptural language – both differences in degree of abstraction and differences in the physique of the forms: Moore's career has not had periods within which he concentrates for a time on one preoccupation to the exclusion of others. Thus the two works which, I believe, dominate this exhibition – and, I believe, are also the most imaginative, most powerful and most personal images that Moore has ever created – the *Sheep Piece* and the *Hill Arches* – look about as different from each other as an elephant and a tiger. It is therefore impossible to generalise comprehensively about the nature of Moore's achievement in the period covered. Nevertheless, I believe that there has been a dominant preoccupation during this period – though *Hill Arches* is among the works not covered by it – a preoccupation which has been manifest in Moore's sculpture only over the last twenty-odd years but in the light of which it is possible to perceive a clear overall pattern in the extreme complexity of his total development. It is a preoccupation implicit in a passage from a conversation with Warren Forma in the early 1960s.

> 'One of the things I would like to think my sculpture has is a force, is a strength, is a life, a vitality from inside it, so that you have a sense that the form is pressing from inside trying to burst or trying to give off the strength from inside itself, rather than having something which is just shaped from outside and stopped. It's as though you have something trying to make itself come to a shape from inside itself. This is, perhaps, what makes me interested in bones as much as in flesh because the bone is the inner structure of all living form. It's the bone that pushes out from inside; as you bend your leg the knee gets tautness over it, and it's there that the movement and the energy come from. If you clench a knuckle, you clench a fist, you get in that sense the bones, the knuckles pushing through, giving a force that if you open your hand and just have it relaxed you don't feel. And so the knee, the shoulder, the skull, the forehead, the part where from inside you get a sense of pressure of the bone outwards – these for me are the key points.'

Back in 1937 Moore wrote a long and carefully thought-out statement which has remained his most thorough and coherent declaration of aims. There are several points made in it on which his thinking has changed, but on the whole it continues to define in a striking way his stance as an artist (for example, there is one short passage which in three sentences seems to encapsulate that whole anti-doctrinaire, anti-extremist, blithely commonsensical attitude that is so deeply ingrained in him: 'The violent quarrel between the abstractionists and the surrealists seems to me quite unnecessary. All good art has contained both abstract and surrealist elements, just as it has contained both classical and romantic elements – order and surprise, intellect and imagination, conscious and unconscious. Both sides of the artist's personality must play their part'). In the course of this essay Moore speaks of the 'special mission' of one of his great progenitors and goes on to define an aspiration which, from a viewpoint forty years on, can be seen as indubitably his own special mission.

> 'Since the Gothic, European sculpture had become overgrown with moss, weeds – all sorts of surface excrescences which completely concealed shape. It has been Brancusi's special mission to get rid of this overgrowth, and to make us once more shape-conscious. To do this he has had to concentrate on very simple direct shapes, to keep his sculpture, as it were, one-cylindered, to refine and polish a single shape to a degree almost too precious. Brancusi's work, apart from its individual value, has been of historical importance in the development of contemporary sculpture. But it may now be no longer necessary to close down and restrict sculpture to the single (static) form unit. We can now begin to open out. To relate and combine together several forms of varied sizes, sections and directions into one organic whole.'

He was saying that complex forms, provided they could be managed, were more interesting than simple forms – in contradiction to the widespread twentieth-century doctrine that 'less is more'. Moore's mission, then, as he saw it, was to restore to European sculpture a traditional richness that had gone bad, had therefore had to be sacrificed during a period of purification, but now had to be recovered.

One of the most profoundly modern things about modern art has been its radically new view of the past. Previously Western artists saw the Western tradition, stemming from classical Greek and Roman sculpture, as their norm; even when they admired and imitated something in the art of other traditions, they thought of these as exotic. This century's attitude is exemplified by a text of Moore's, published in 1941, in which he looked back to his frequent visits to the British Museum as a student and, following a discussion of various forms of 'primitive art' – as it was still called then – went on:

> 'But underlying these individual characteristics, these featural peculiarities in the primitive schools, a common world-language of form is apparent in them all; through the working of instinctive sculptural sensibility, the same shapes and form relationships are used to express similar ideas at widely different places and periods in history, so that the same form-vision may be seen in a Negro and a Viking carving, a Cycladic stone figure and a Nukuoro wooden statuette. And on further familiarity with the British

> Museum's whole collection it eventually became clear to me that the realistic ideal of physical beauty in art which sprang from fifth-century Greece was only a digression from the main world tradition of sculpture, whilst, for instance, our own equally European Romanesque and early Gothic are in the main line.'

The same way of thinking is implicit in a list which Moore had set out in an article in 1935 of what seemed to him 'the great sculpture of the world': Sumerian, early Greek, Etruscan, Ancient Mexican, Fourth and Twelfth Dynasty Egyptian, Romanesque, early Gothic.

Now, virtually all the sculpture for which Moore professes admiration in these writings is compact, four-square, *frontal*. Yet frontality is fundamentally incompatible with Moore's desire 'to relate and combine together several forms of varied sizes, sections and directions' – *directions* is the operative word – a desire clearly manifest in his work from the time of his first mature pieces, in the late 1920s. At the same time, the tendency to make sculpture that relates and combines forms varying in direction has been what above all has distinguished the European tradition – from fifth-century Greece to Michelangelo, Bernini and Rodin – from the kinds of tribal and archaic art which Moore placed in 'the main world tradition of sculpture'. In his practice as an artist Moore reveals a profound instinctive allegiance to the classical and Renaissance tradition. The clearest demonstration of this is his strong preference for the reclining figure as a theme: among all his sculptures of complete figures, at least two-thirds are reclining figures. And the reclining figure is virtually a prerogative of the European tradition. Among the few examples of reclining figures to be found in archaic or tribal sculpture are the representations of the Mexican rain-god, Chac-mool, and it is well known that one of these statues was the main source for Moore's early reclining figures. Yet even here Moore modifies his prototype in ways that specifically suggest the countervailing influence of Michelangelo.

Moore's art, then, has always been more or less involved in reconciling certain modernist assumptions with the European tradition against which modernism has rebelled; throughout most of his career he has tended to give his sculpture the sort of complexity of articulation which that tradition has nourished in preference to the sort of iconic intensity – closely bound up with frontality – achieved by Egyptian and Sumerian and Cycladic and African sculpture. There is another attribute which is somewhat the prerogative of the European tradition: that the illusory surface tension of a sculpture presents decided contrasts between hard passages and soft passages. There is little of this kind of contrast in archaic and tribal sculpture; there is little of it in twentieth-century sculpture. It begins to appear in Moore's sculpture in the mid-1950s, with transitions as violent as they are in Rodin where an exceedingly taut, bone-hard passage moves abruptly into a relaxed, resilient, fleshy passage, conveying dramatically 'a sense that the form is pressing from inside trying to burst . . . a sense of pressure of the bone outwards'.

The hard/soft contrast first appears in small semi-abstract works, many of them reliefs but also one maquette of 1954 for a reclining figure, quite different in character from others made at the time, which became the model for the earliest work in our exhibition, the grand *Reclining Figure* (Plates 2 and 3) in elm wood carved between 1959 and 1964. In the meantime Moore had produced other large-scale works with hard/soft form, on the one hand the decidedly figurative *Seated Woman* and *Falling Warrior*, on the other the decidedly abstract series of *Upright Motives* (including the *Glenkiln Cross*). From the time of its appearance in Moore's work, hard/soft form was present in certain works at every point in his gamut of styles, and it is present in a majority of exhibits here.

The emphasis Moore places on the contrast between hard and soft passages seems to me to relate to an increasing preoccupation with tactile sensations and motor sensations rather than visual ones. These sculptures show forth the experience of running one's hands over a body – and into a body – responding to the shapes of its bones and their marvellous thinness, to its blindly-perceived landscape of hollows and bumps, to the resistance of bone and muscle, the give of flesh and membrane. And they show forth what is experienced in using one's body, feeling one's skin stretching tautly over one's knuckles as one clenches a fist, feeling the muscles tighten as one extends a limb. These hard/soft sculptures are haptic images: they make bodies – or parts of bodies – look the way they feel, from outside and from inside.

Bodies or parts of bodies: especially parts, perhaps, in that tactile and motor experiences focus on parts of the body. But there can be a marvellous uncertainty about what part is involved. And Moore's haptic metaphors are resonant with ambiguities. 'To make a shape strongly significant, without knowing why, or why it is so,' he wrote in a recent notebook, and added: 'Perhaps ability to do this comes about because of the sculptor's intense interest in all forms and shapes – through empathy and human connections.'

It has to do, in a way, with sculpting like a blind man. The *Sheep Piece* (Plates 22 and 23) is the epitome of this and a perfect counterpart to the more visual *Hill Arches* (Plates 24, 25, 26 and 27). *Hill Arches*, with its flamboyant energy, its superb symmetry, its coiled tension, its predatory menace, its formality and its sheer magnificence, is like an especially ritualistic and flashy mating display. The *Sheep Piece* is, to begin with, a beast mounting another. This is a quiet, rather secretive, sort of mating and the relationship between the creatures also suggests an asexual longing of bodies for contact with others, like the nuzzling of blind puppies – the converse of the erotic overtones of the *Mother and Child* (Plates 10 and 11) in rosa aurora marble of 1967. And beyond this there is a still more universal, elemental sense of a blind, helpless need to live and to touch. Sculpture as expressive as this of the primacy of the tactile celebrates the fact that, whether we make love with the lights off or the lights on, the crucial contact happens in the dark.

MAQUETTES AND NATURAL OBJECTS

In addition to the works listed in the catalogue, the exhibition includes a selection of about a hundred of the artist's plaster maquettes. These are shown – as they are in his studio – mingled with some of the found objects which have been a major source of inspiration: shells, flints, pebbles, bones 'saved out of the stew-pot', animal skulls from the butcher's shop which once stood on part of his garden.

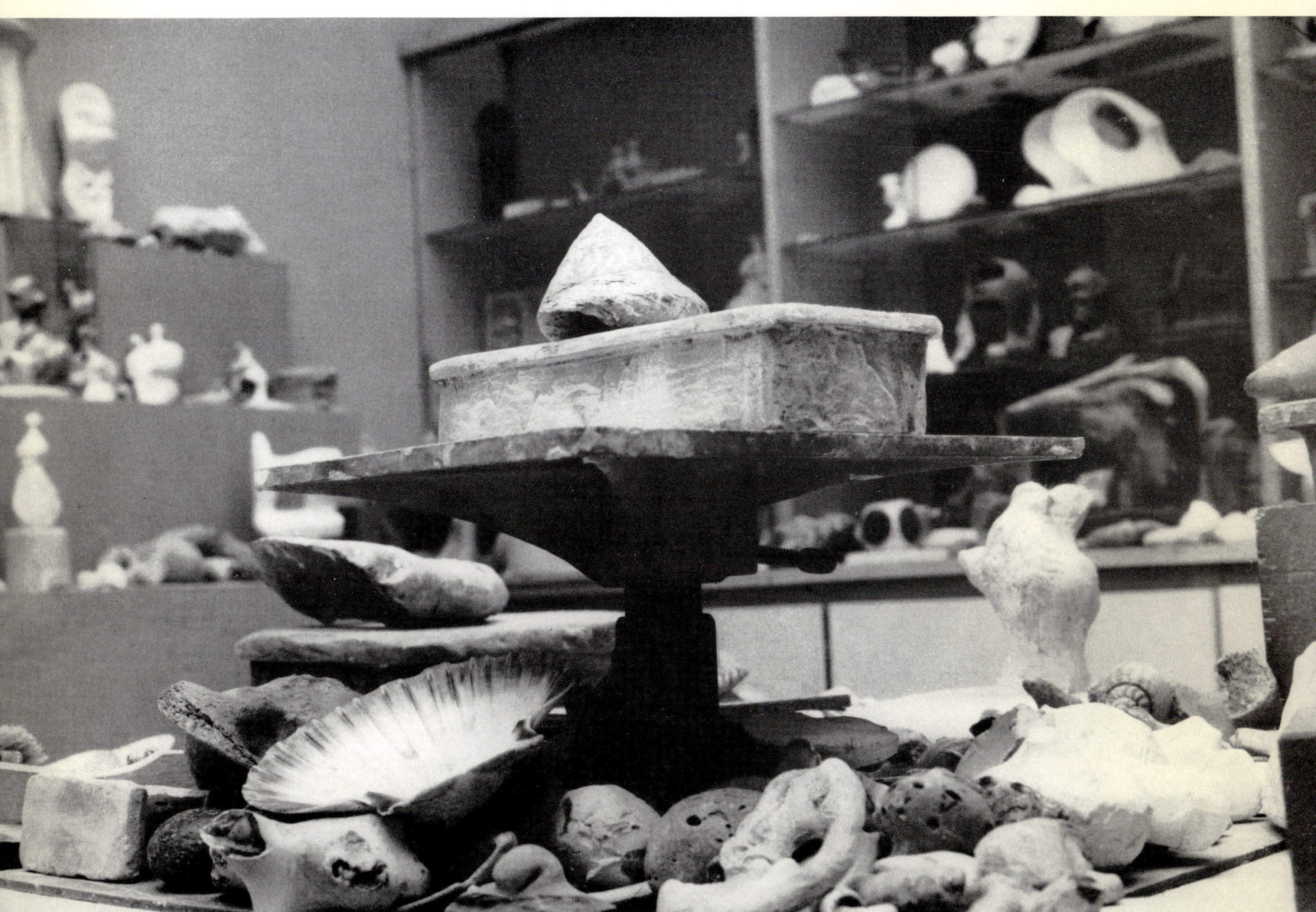

Plate A

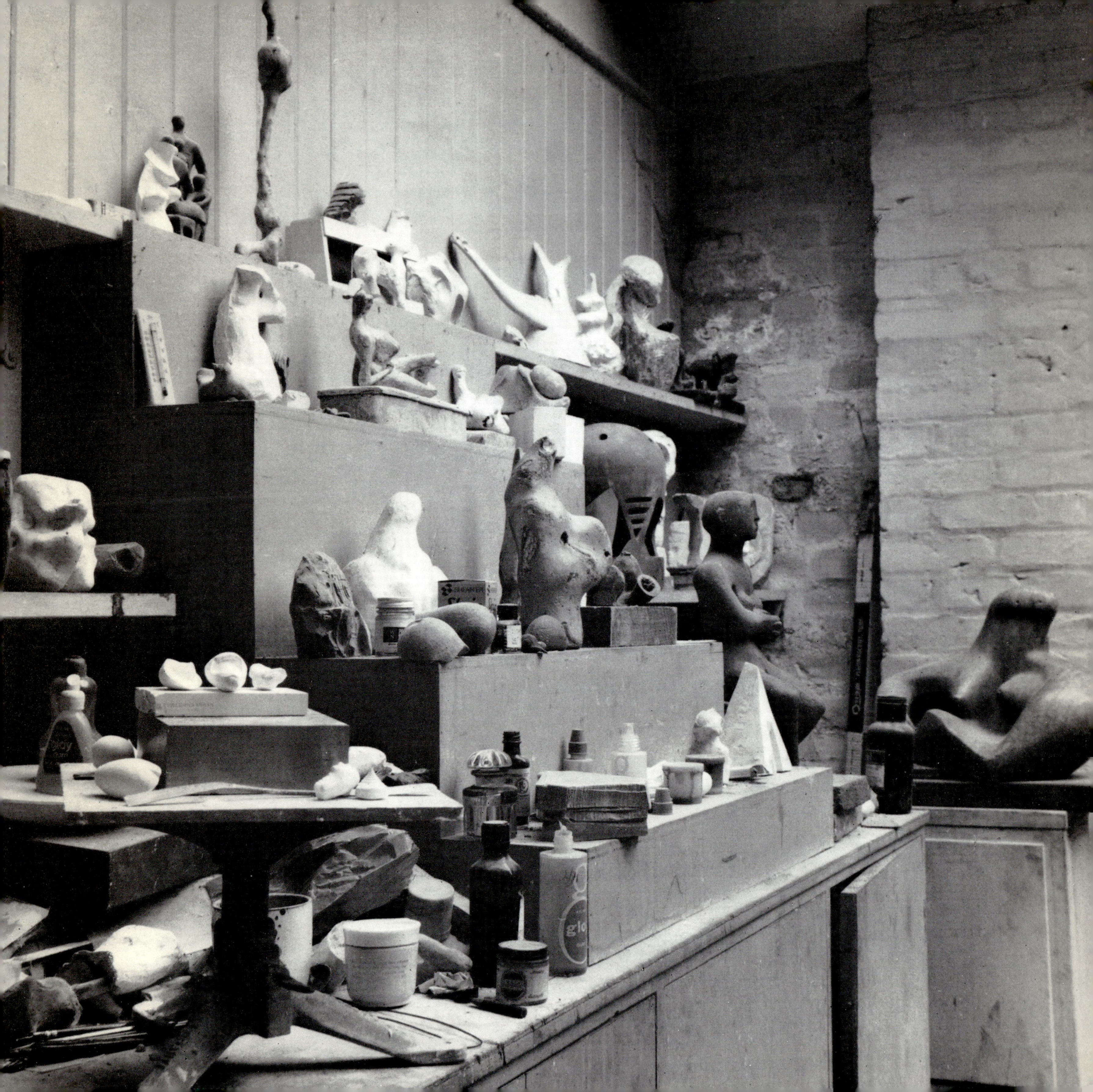

'When I first began doing sculpture about 1922 or so, I often worked direct in a piece of stone or wood, which might have been not a geometric shape but just an odd random block of stone that one found cheaply in some stonemason's yard, or a log of wood which was a natural shape, and then I'd make a sculpture, trying to get as big a sculpture out of that bit of material as I could, and therefore one would wait until the material suggested an idea.

Nowadays I don't work so much in that way, as I have an idea, or an idea comes to me, and then I find the material to make it in, and to do that, the ideas that I am concerned with, I'll produce several maquettes – sketches in plaster – not much bigger than one's hand, certainly small enough to hold in one's hand, so that you can turn them around as you shape them and work on them without having to get up and walk around them, and you have a complete grasp of their shape from all around the whole time. If the form, the idea, that you're doing is much bigger than that, then to see what it's like on the other side, you have to get up, walk around it, and this restricts your imagining and grasping what it's like as you can when it's small. But all the time that I am doing this small model, in my mind it isn't the small model that I'm doing, it's the big sculpture that I intend to do.'

1964

'One doesn't know really how any ideas come. But you can induce them by starting in the far little studio with looking at a box of pebbles. Sometimes I may scribble some doodles, as I said, in a notebook; within my mind they may be a reclining figure, or perhaps a particular subject. Then with those pebbles, or the sketches in the notebook, I sit down and something begins. Then perhaps at a certain stage the idea crystallises and then you know what to do, what to alter. You dislike what you've just made, and change it. At the end of a week you're sitting in that nice little easy chair with the bench in front, and there'll be probably some fifteen or so maquettes about 5 or 6 inches long, if it's a reclining figure, or that height if it's an upright. Then either I know that a few of those are ideas that I like, or that I don't like any of them. If some are ones that I like, then I'll do a variation on that idea, or I'll change it if I'm critical. Done in that way the thing evolves. In my mind always though, in making these little ideas, is the eventual sculpture which may be ten or twelve times the size of the maquette that I hold in my hand.'

1960

'The human figure is what interests me most deeply, but I have found principles of form and rhythm from the study of natural objects such as pebbles, rocks, bones, trees, plants, etc.

Pebbles and rocks show nature's way of working stone. Smooth, sea-worn pebbles show the wearing away, rubbed treatment of stone and principles of asymmetry.

Rocks show the hacked, hewn treatment of stone, and have a jagged nervous block rhythm.

Bones have marvellous structural strength and hard tenseness of form, subtle transition of one shape into the next and great variety in section.

Trees (tree trunks) show principles of growth and strength of joints, with easy passing of one section into the next. They give the ideal for wood sculpture, upward twisting movement.

Shells show nature's hard but hollow form (metal sculpture) and have a wonderful completeness of single shape.'

1933

Plates A, B
The artist's maquette studio

Plate 1 **Reclining Figure: Holes** 1976–78 *length* 2.23m (18) in progress

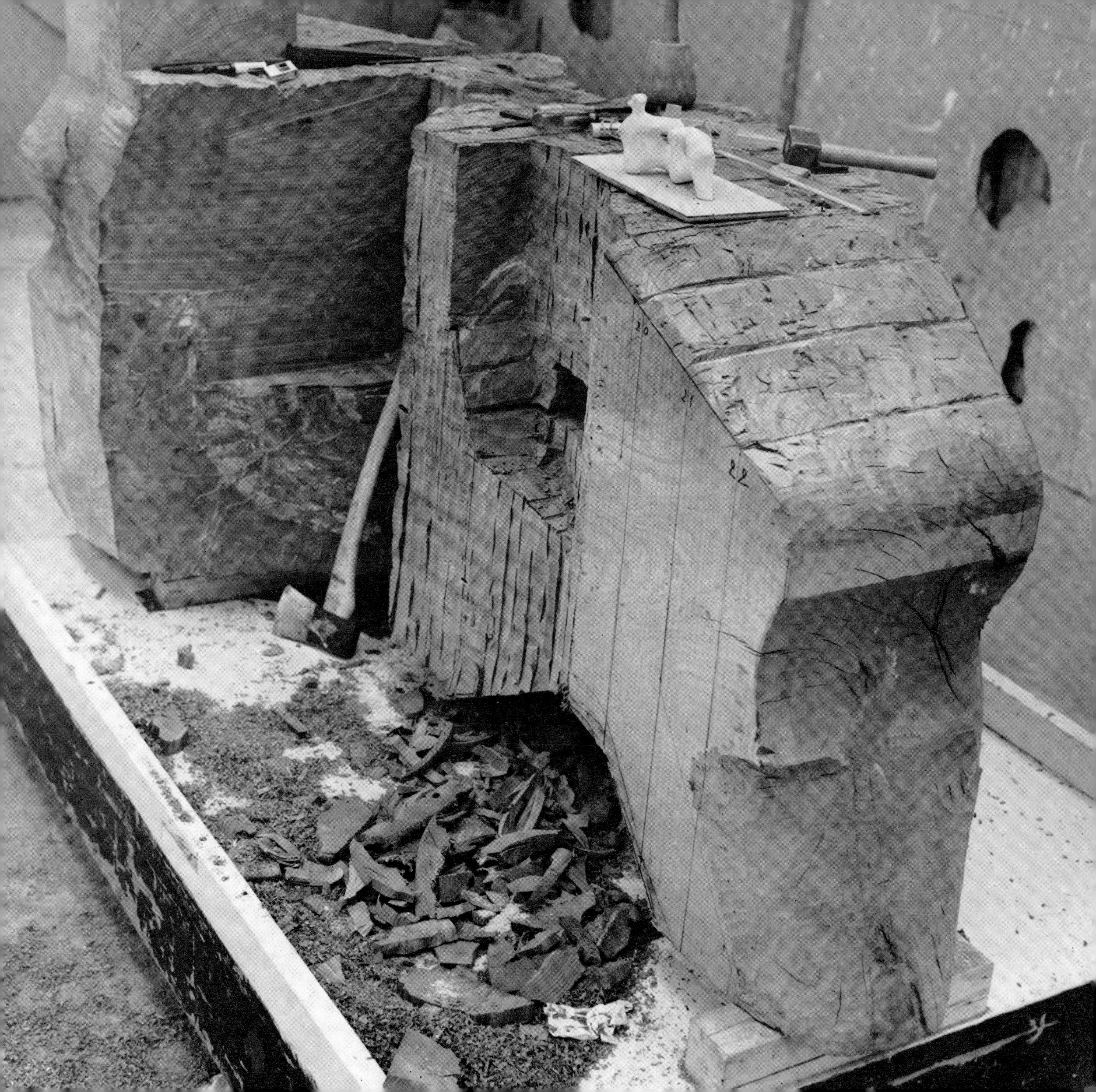

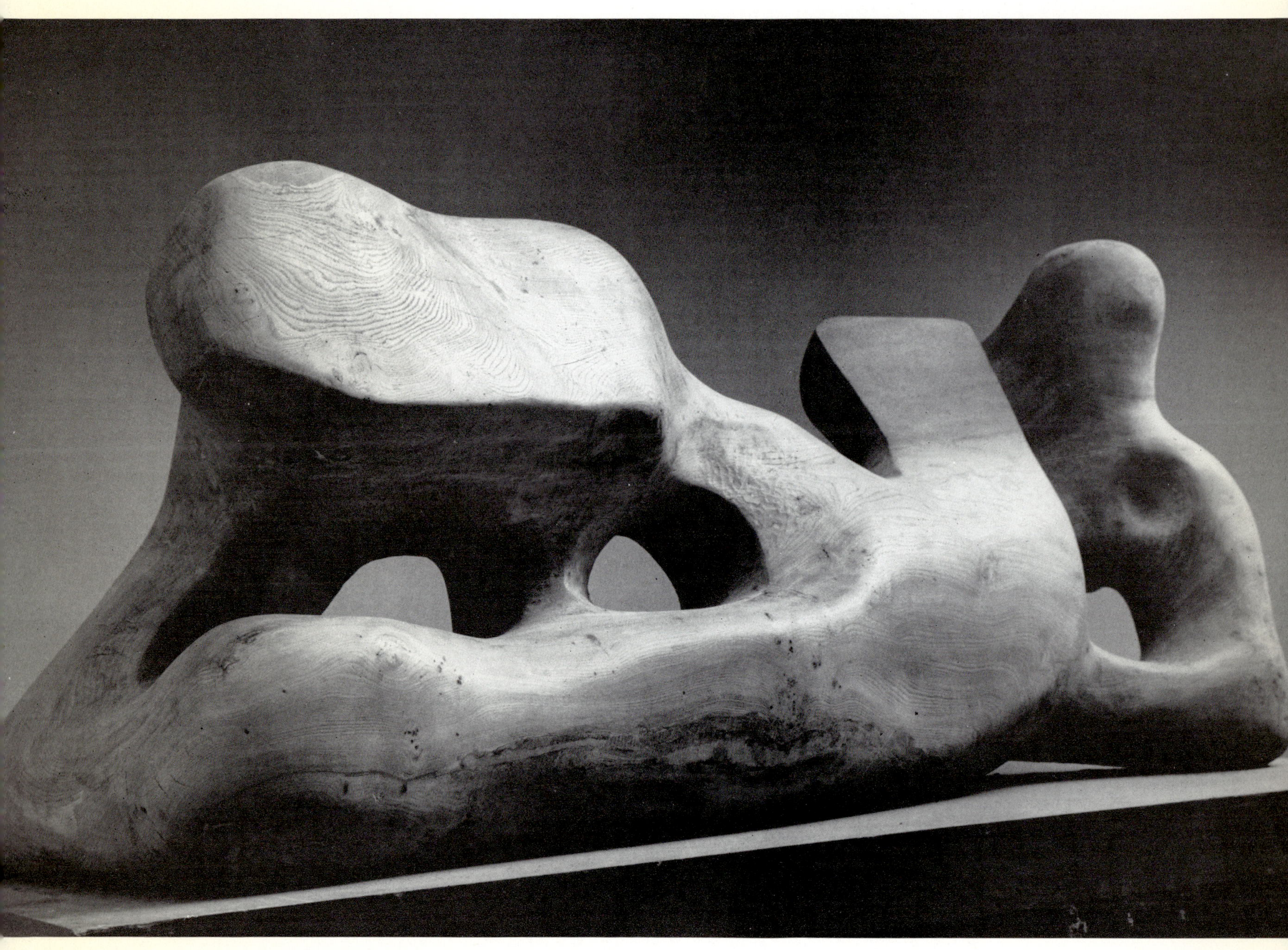

Plates 2, 3 **Reclining Figure** 1959–64 *length* 2.28m (1)

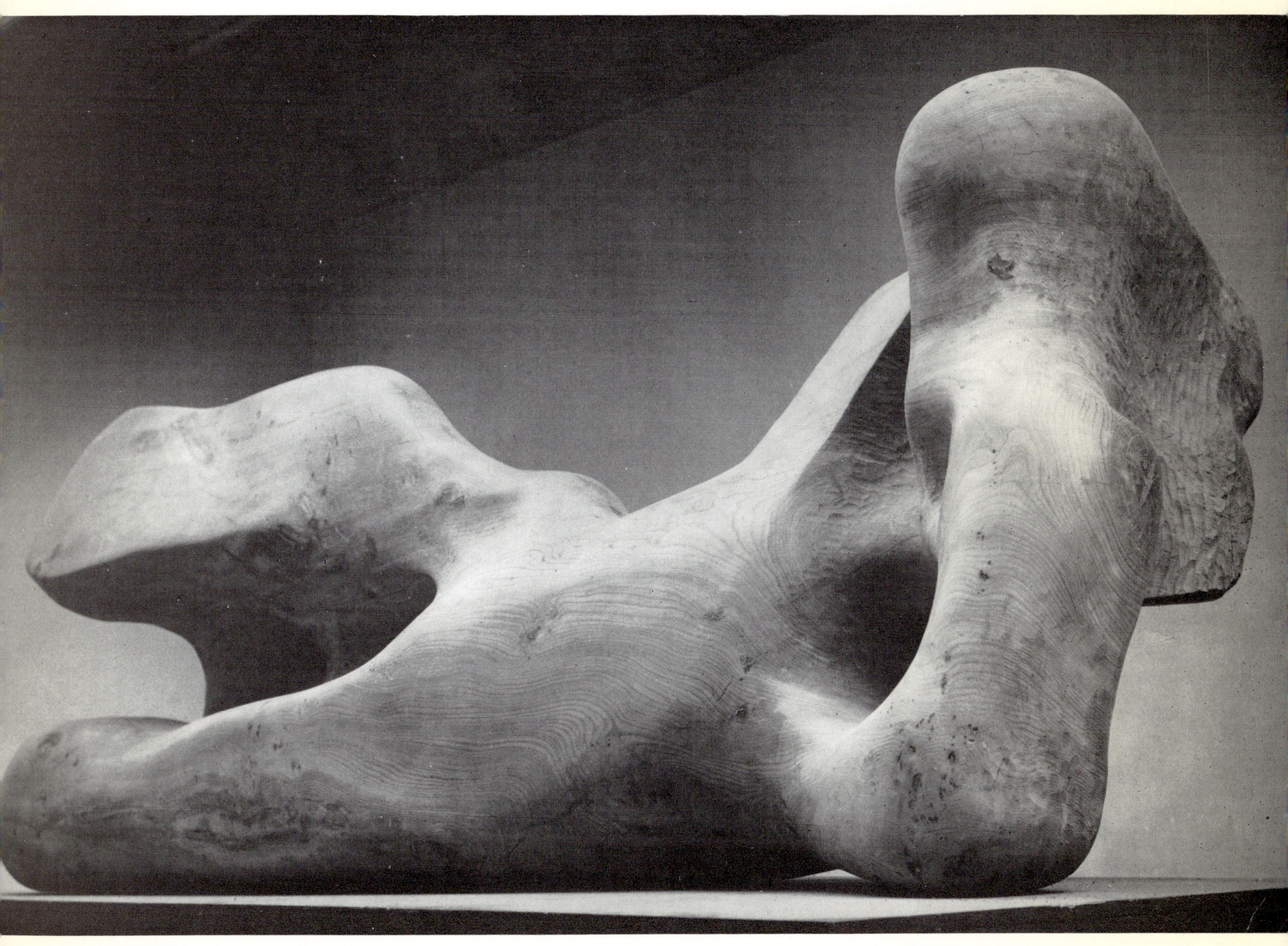

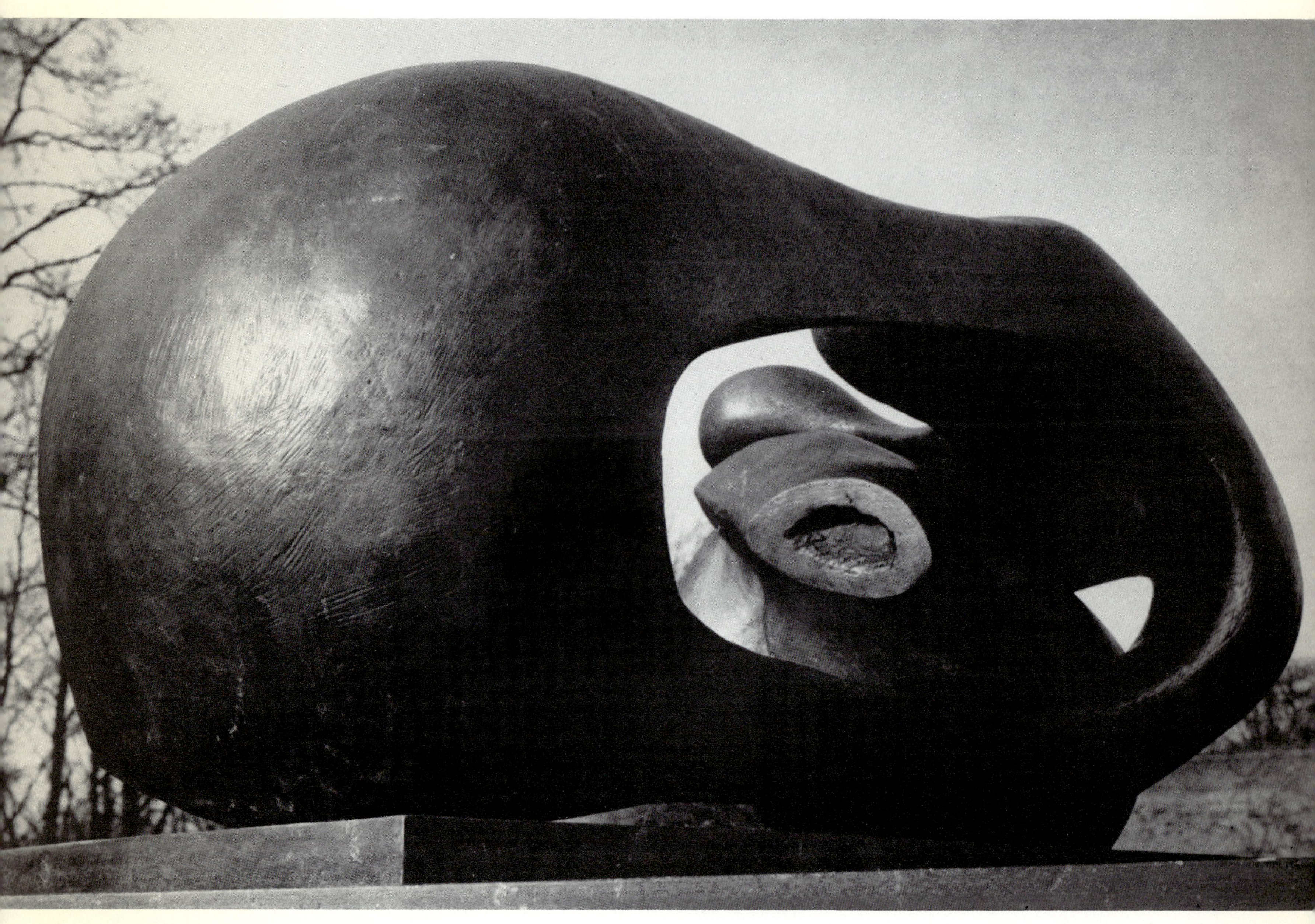

Plates 4, 5 **Reclining Mother and Child** 1960–61 *length* 2.20m (2)

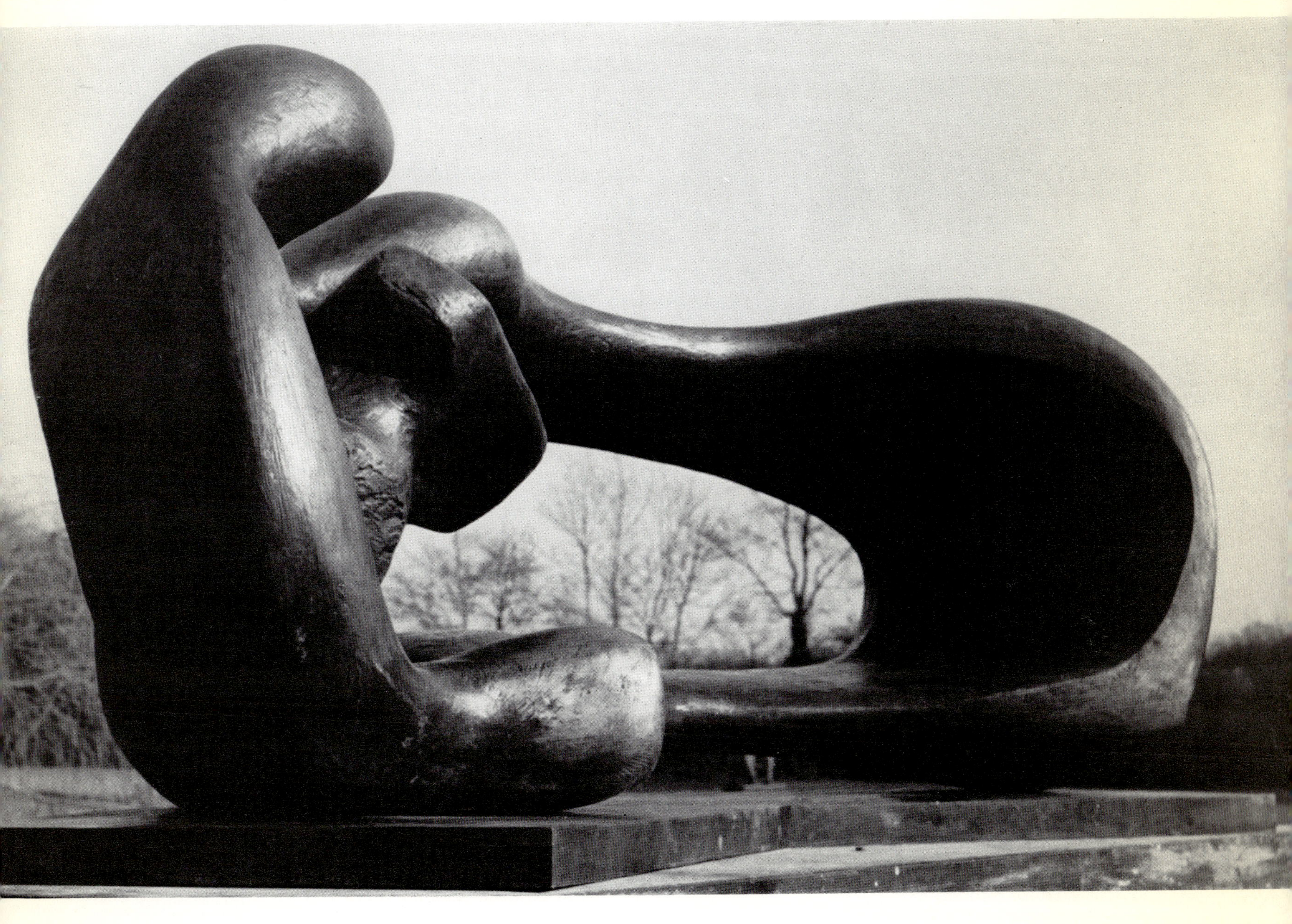

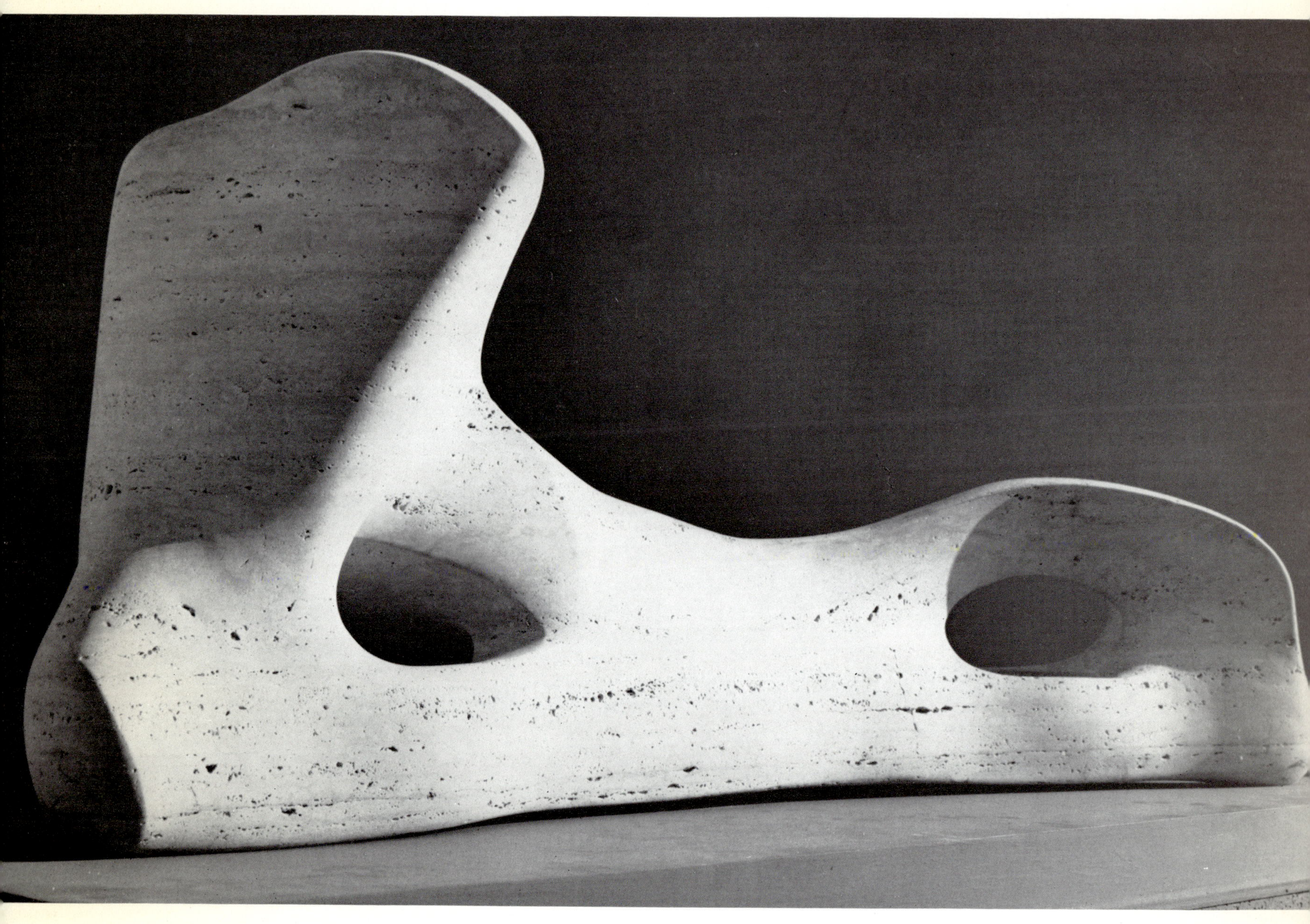

Plate 6 **Reclining Figure: Bone** 1975 *length* 1.57m (15)

Plate 7 **The Arch** 1969 *height* 5.48m (3)

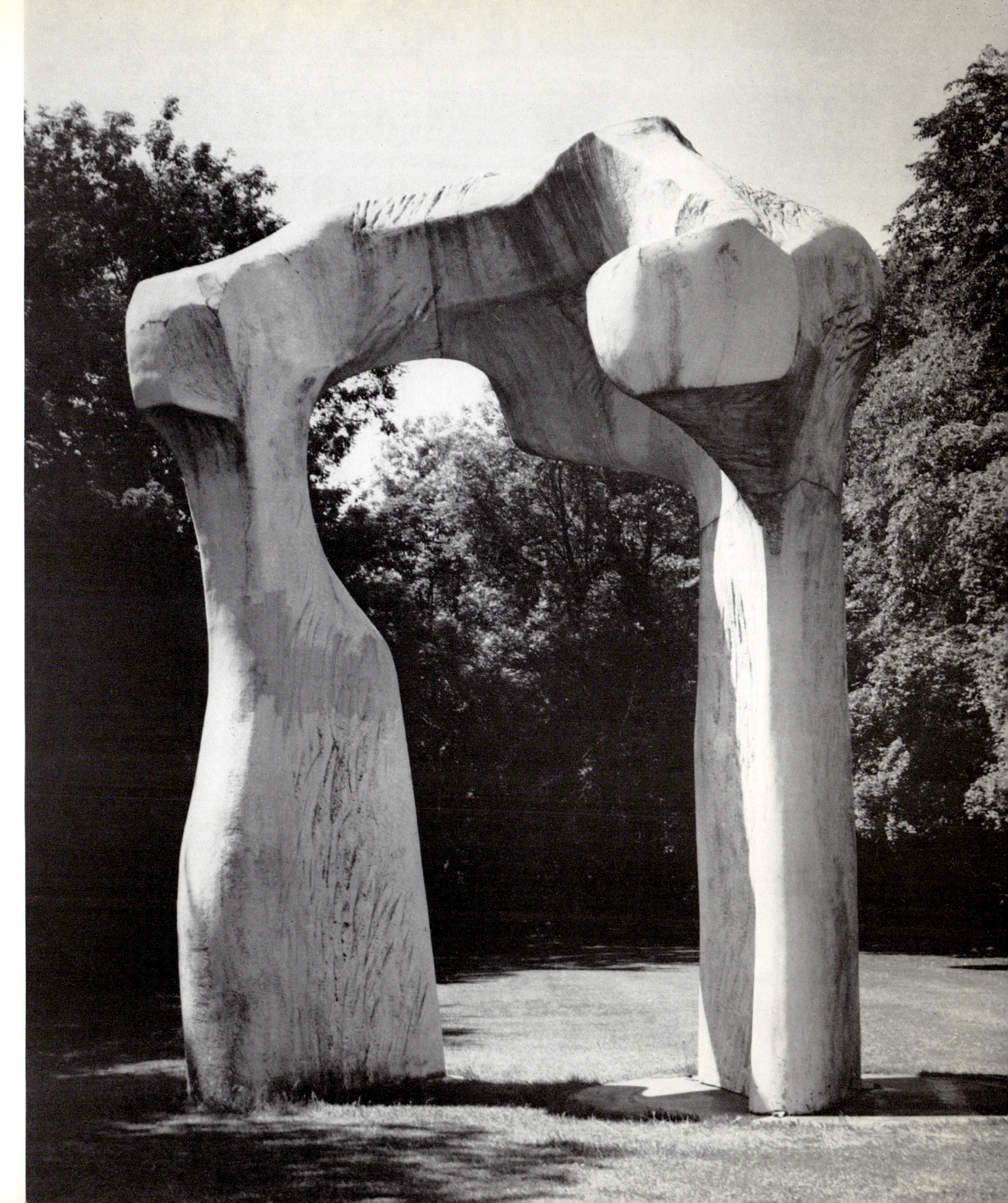

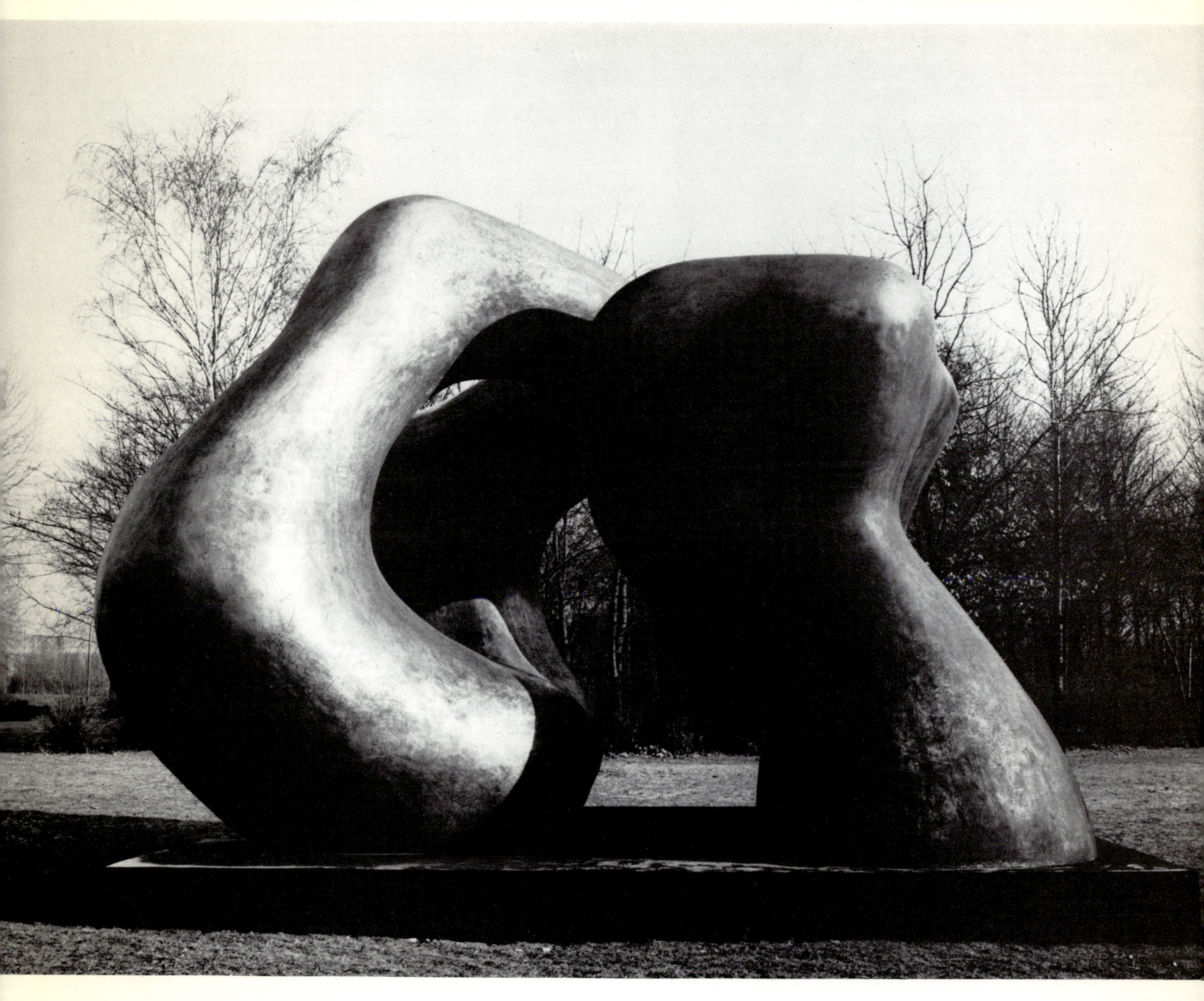

Plates 8, 9 **Large Two Forms** 1969 *length* 6.11m (4)

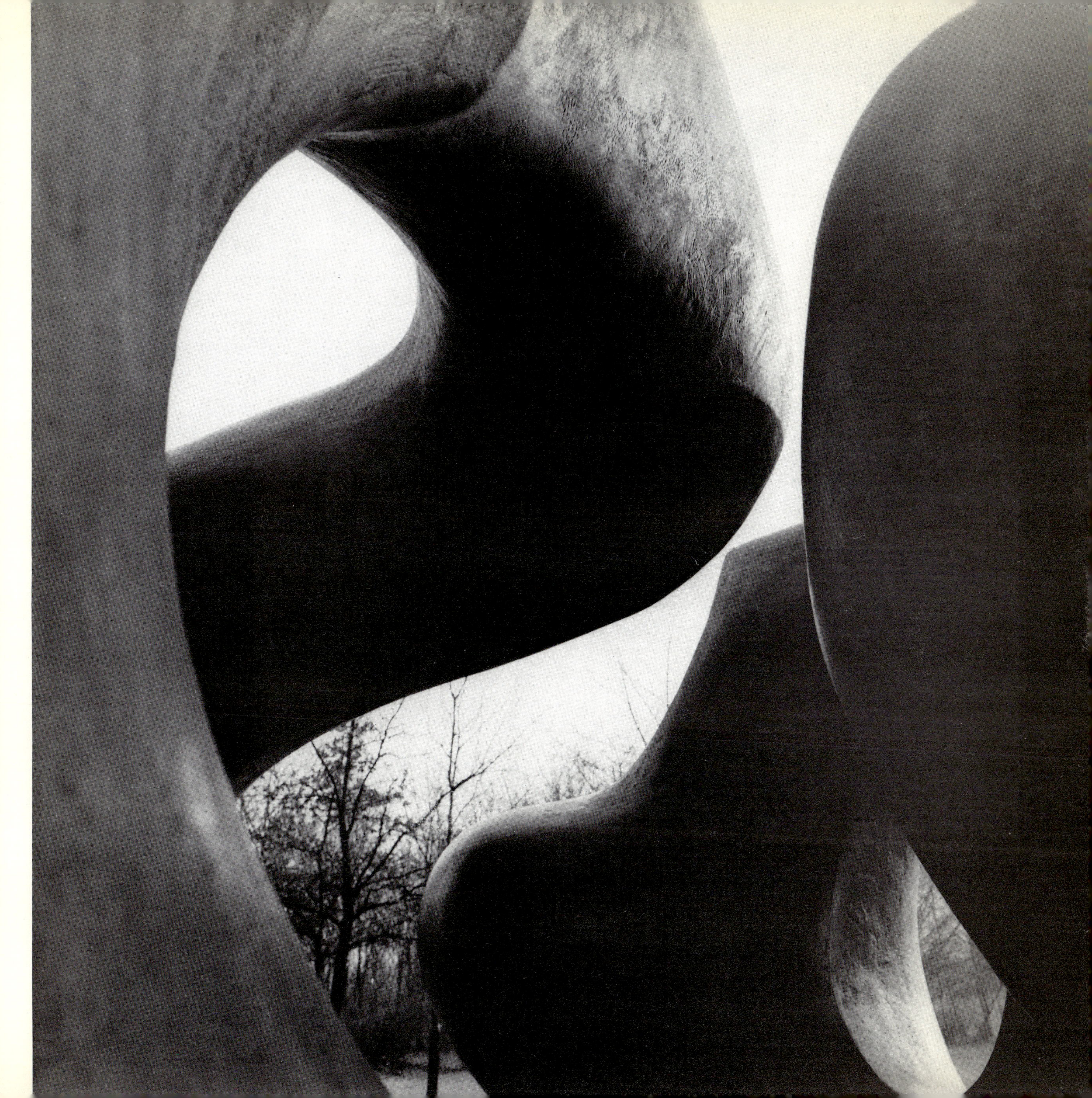

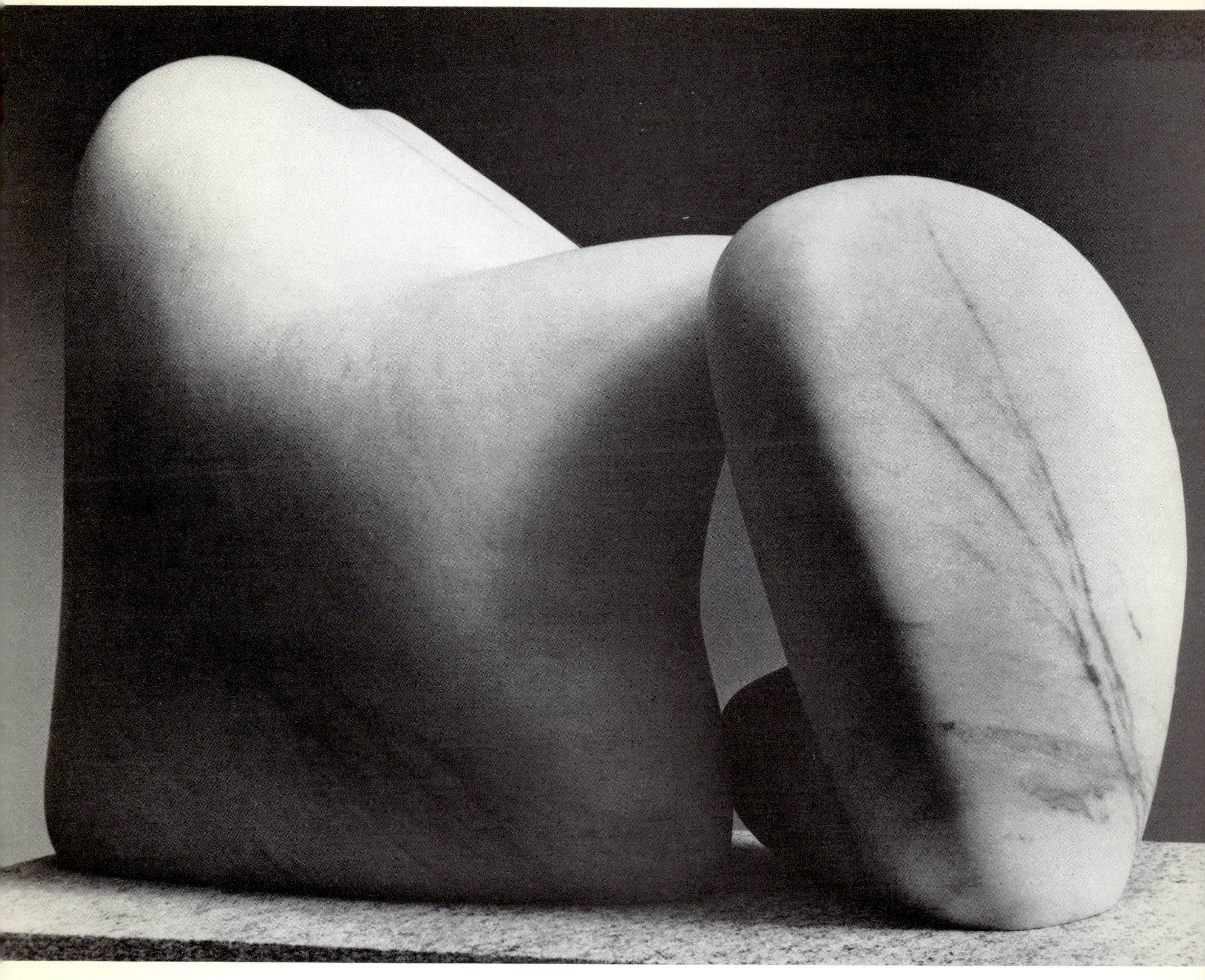

Plates 10, 11 **Mother and Child** 1967 *length* 1.30m (5)

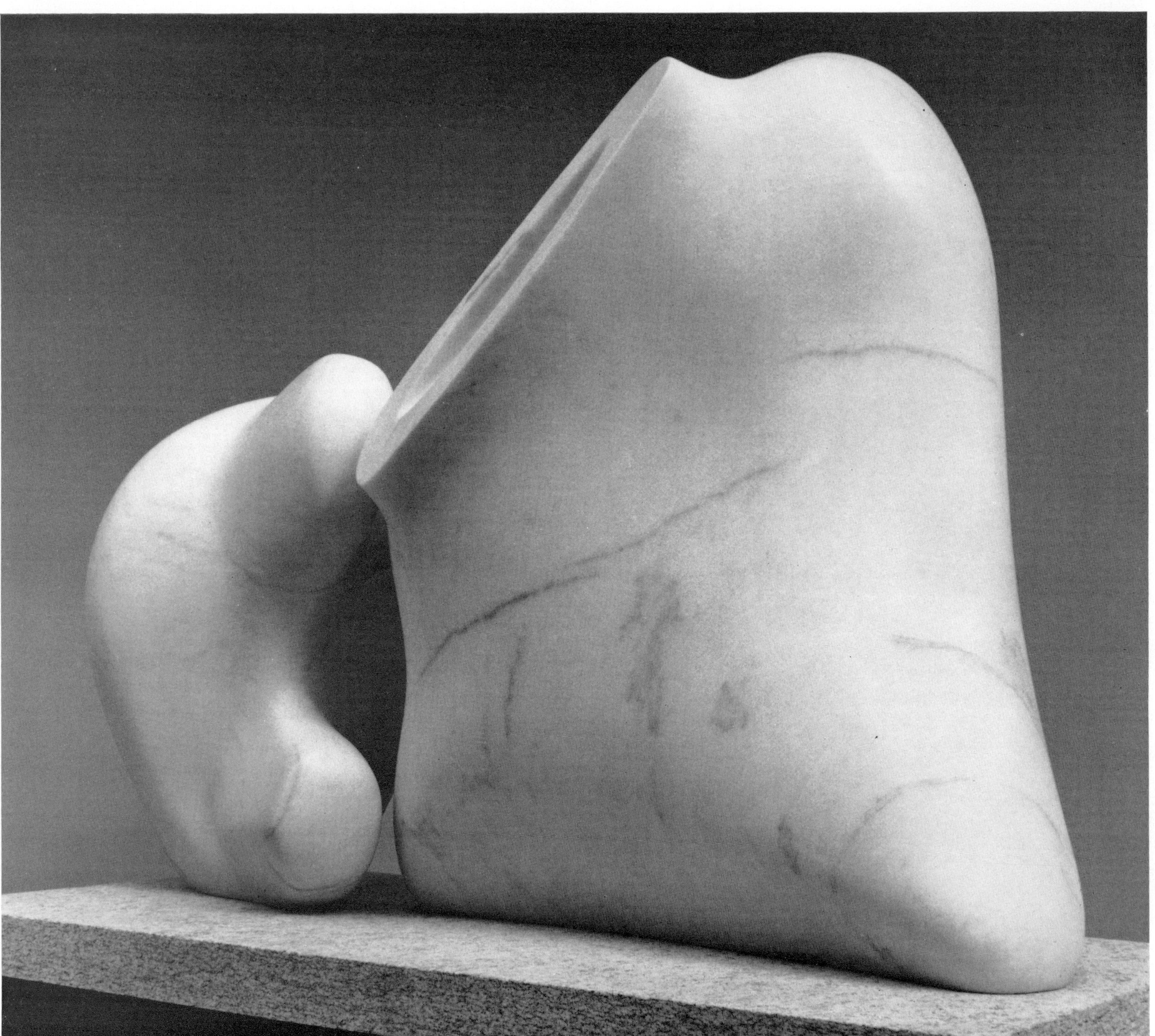

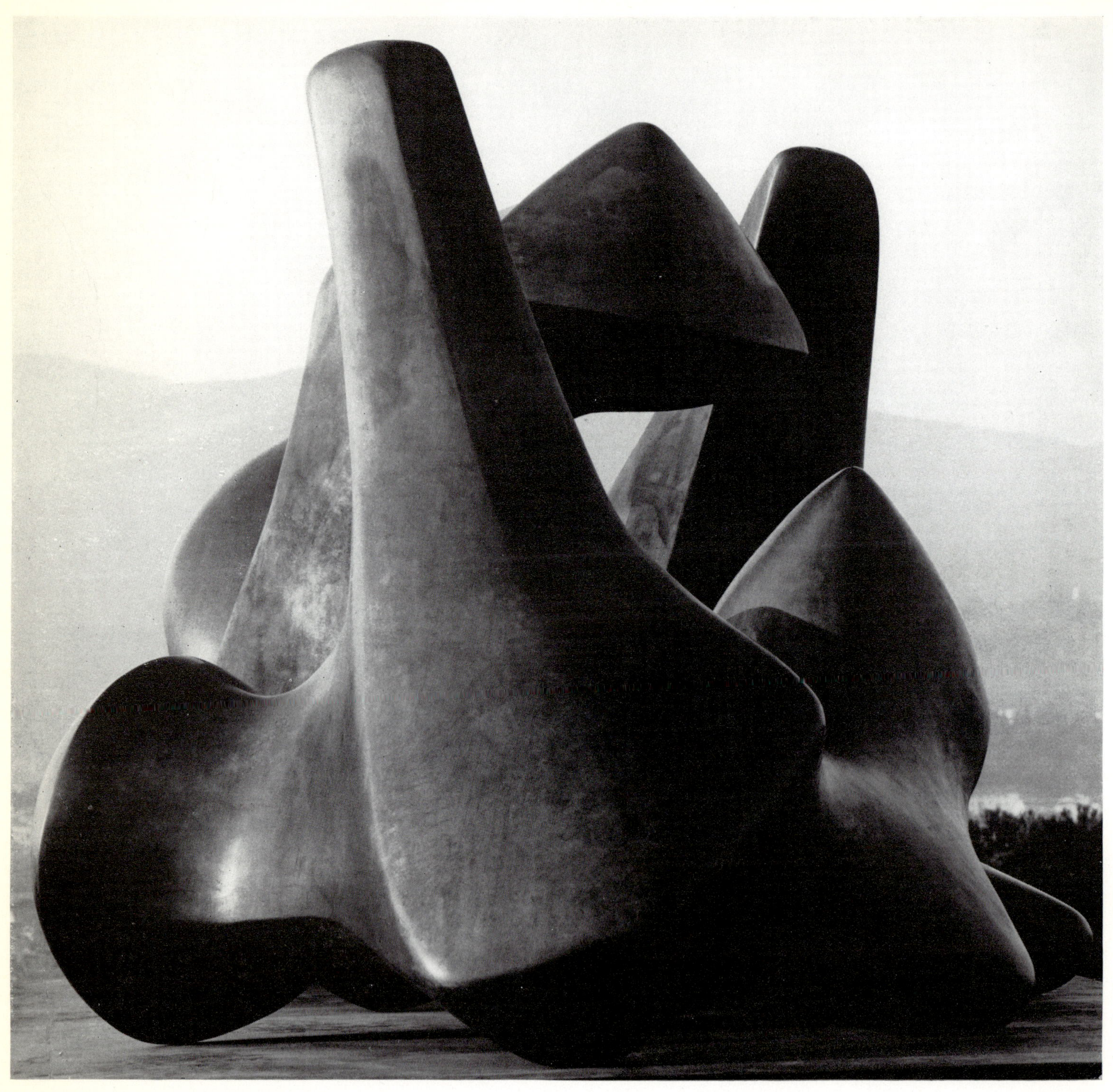

Plates 12, 13 **Three Piece Sculpture: Vertebrae** 1968–69 *length* 6.46m (6)

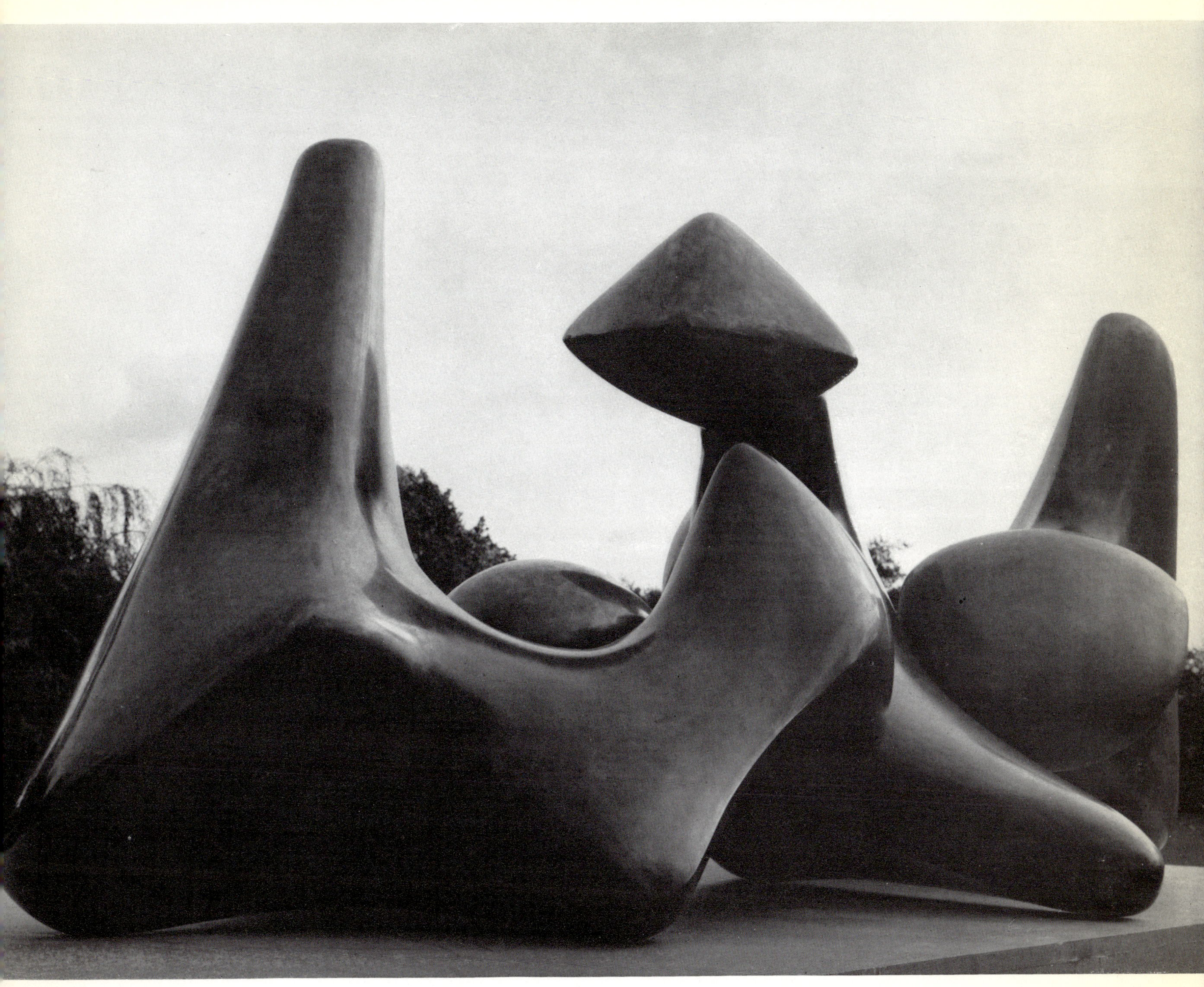

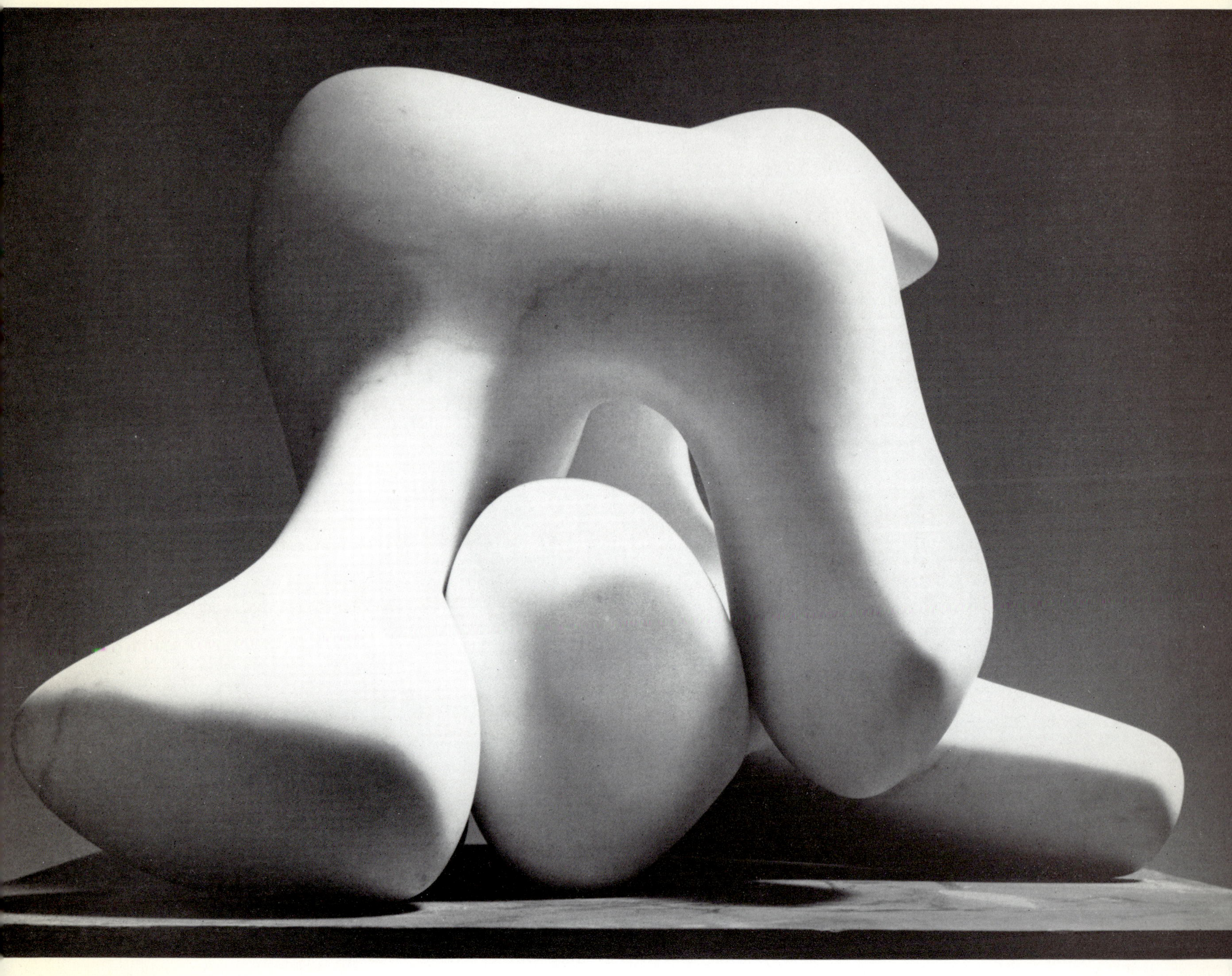

Plates 14, 15 **Two Piece Carving: Interlocking** 1968 *length* 0.71m (7)

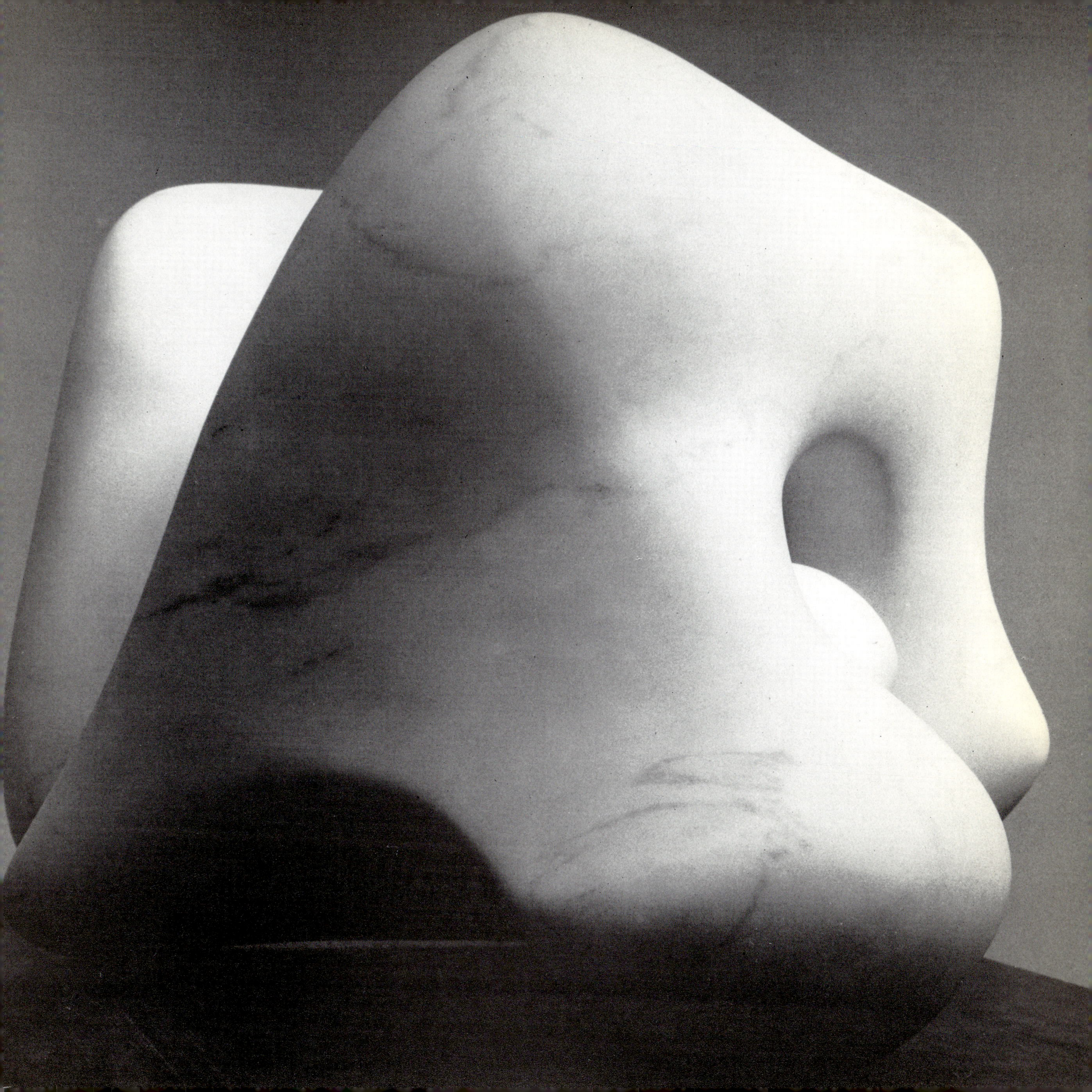

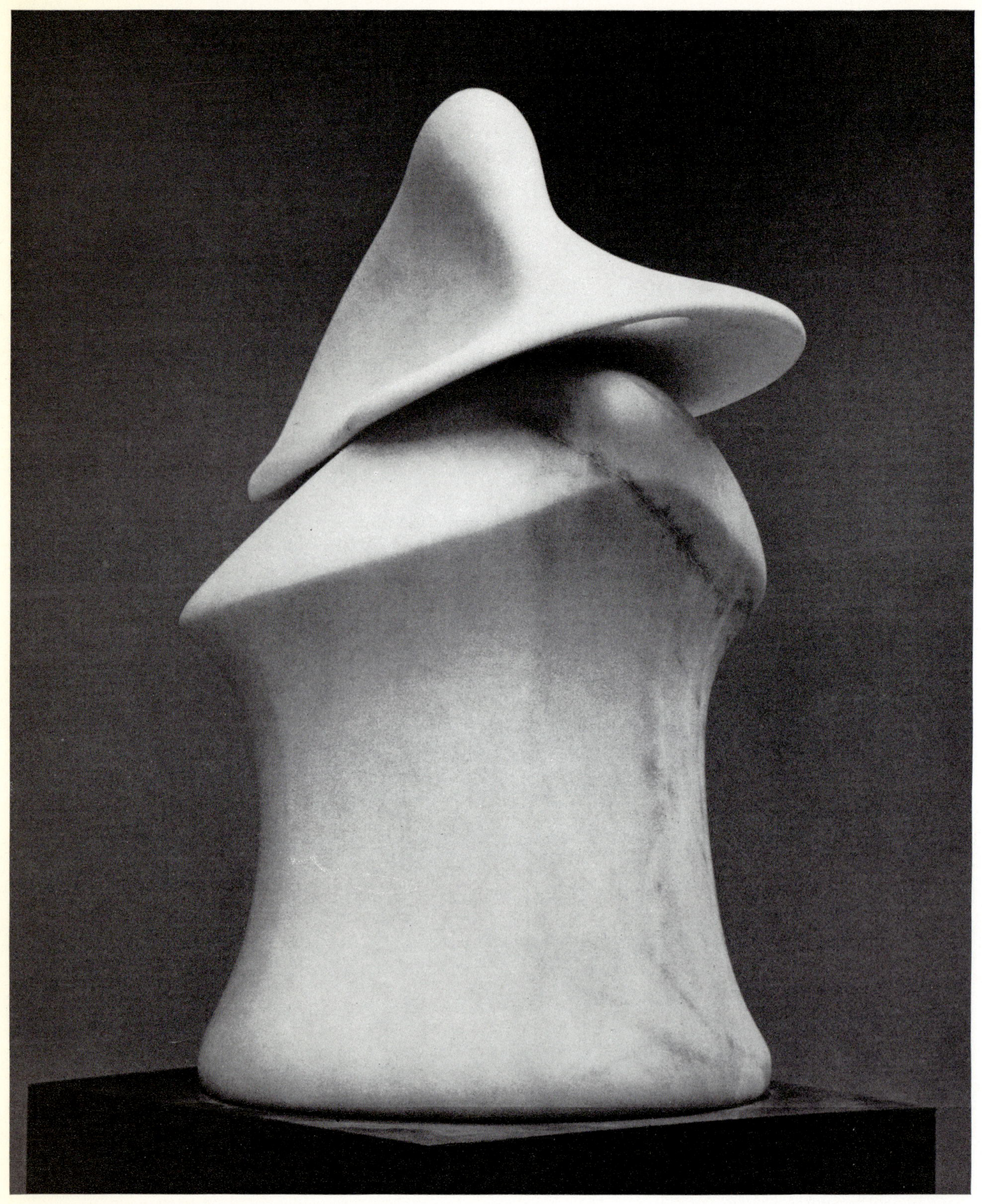

Plate 16 **Bust of a Girl: Two Piece** 1968 *height* 0.78m (8)

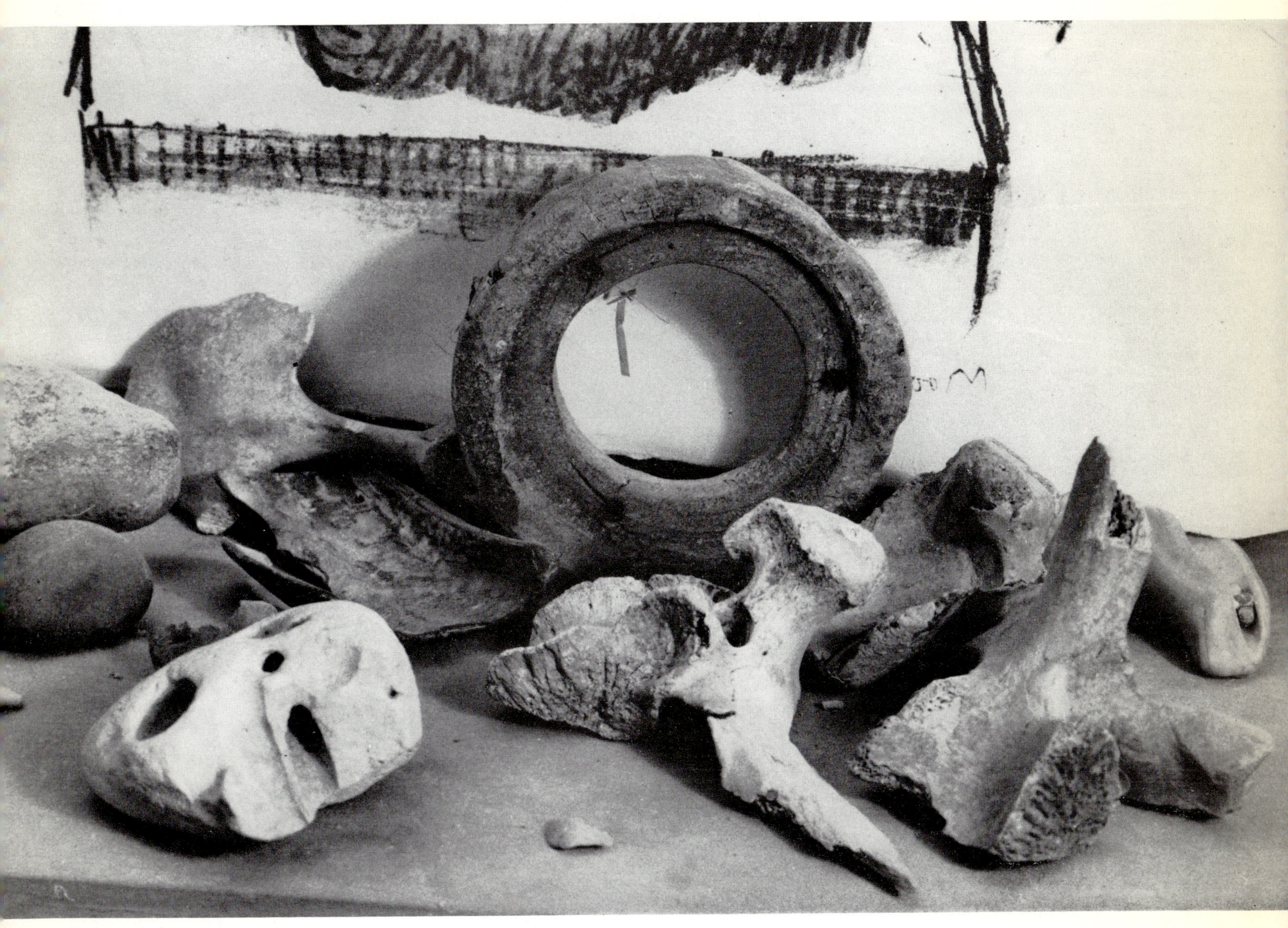

Plate 17 Stones and bones in the artist's studio

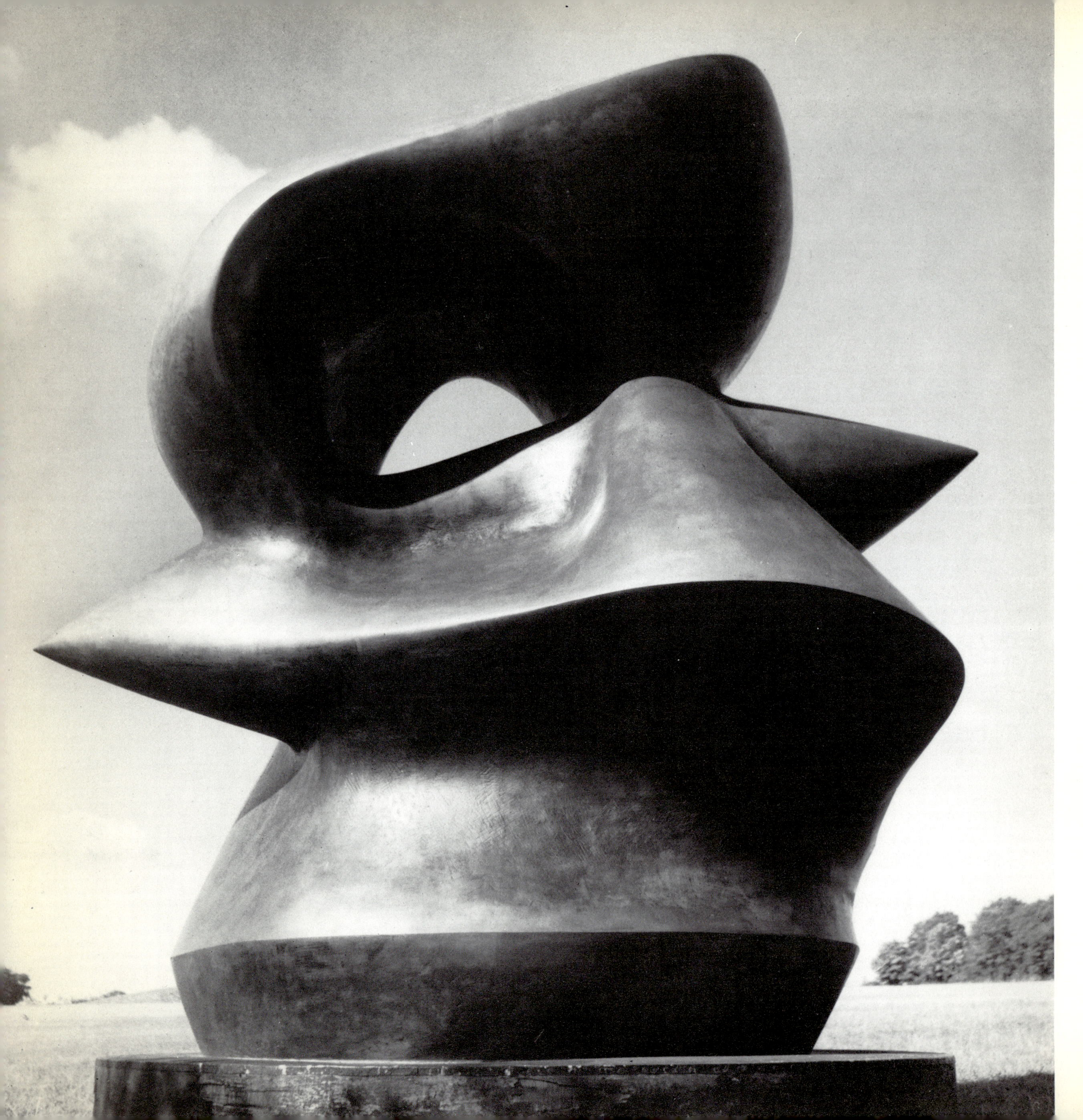

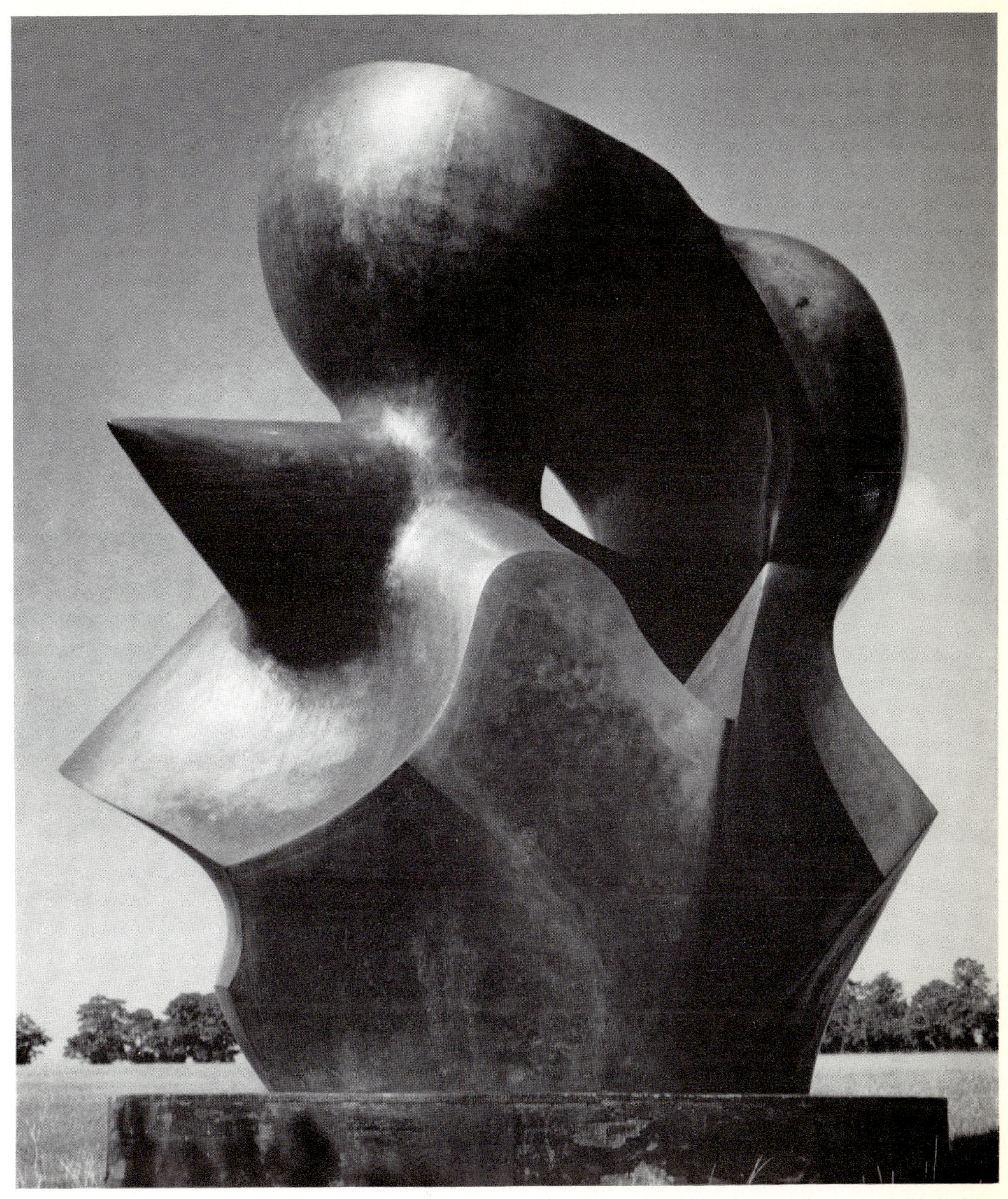

Plates 18, 19 **Large Spindle Piece** 1974 *height* 3.35m (9)

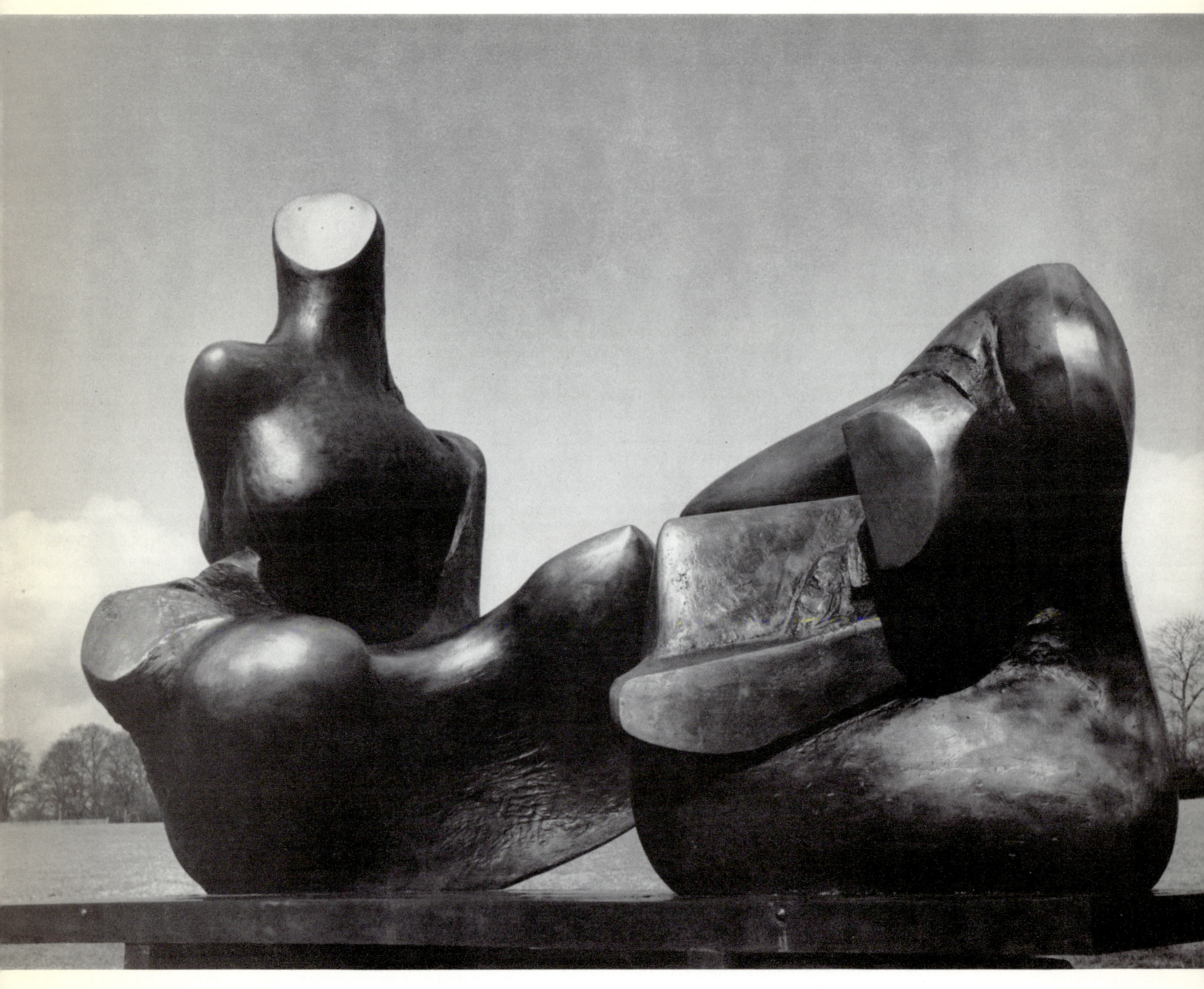

Plates 20, 21 **Two Piece Reclining Figure: Points** 1969–70 *length* 3.66m (10)

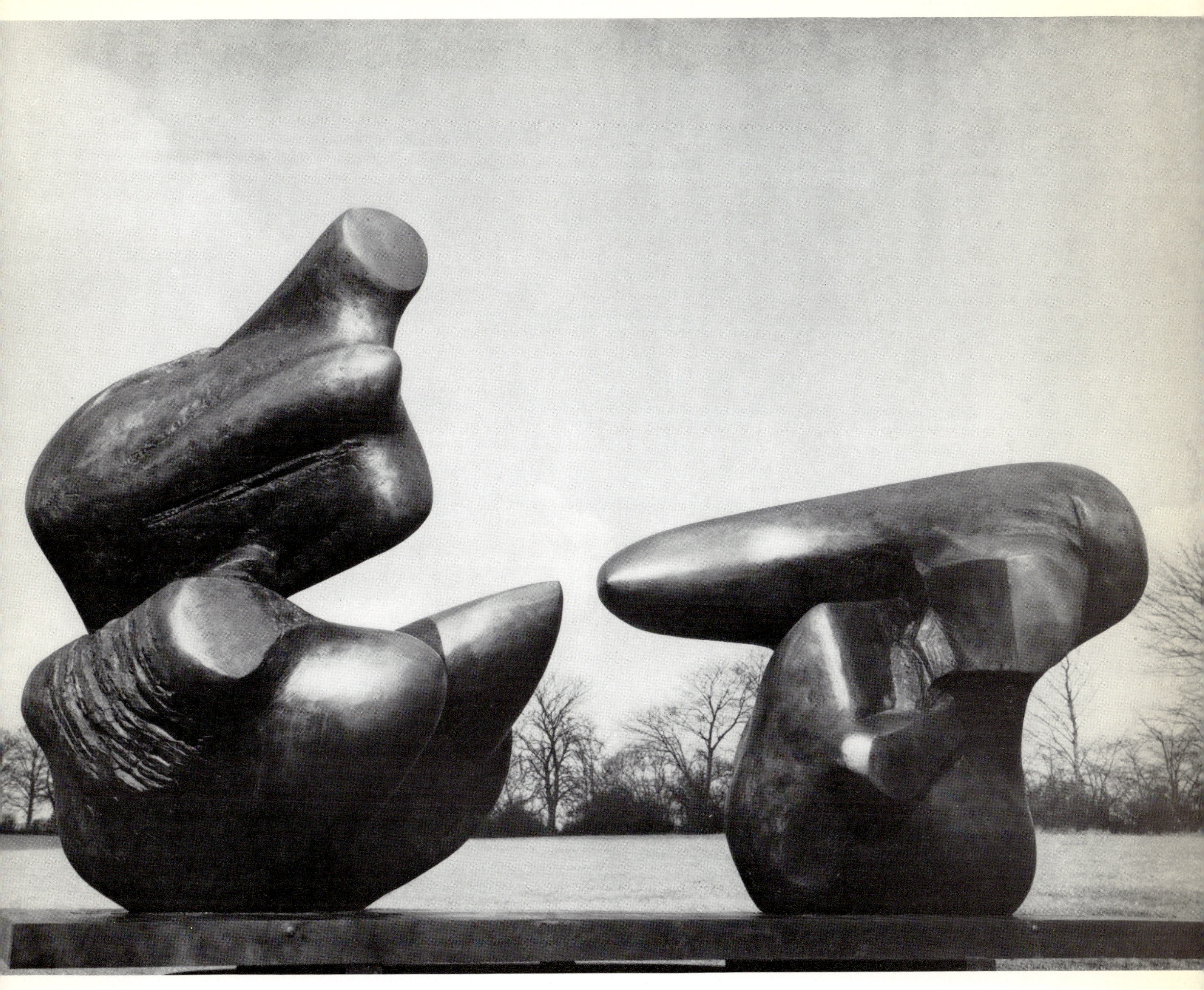

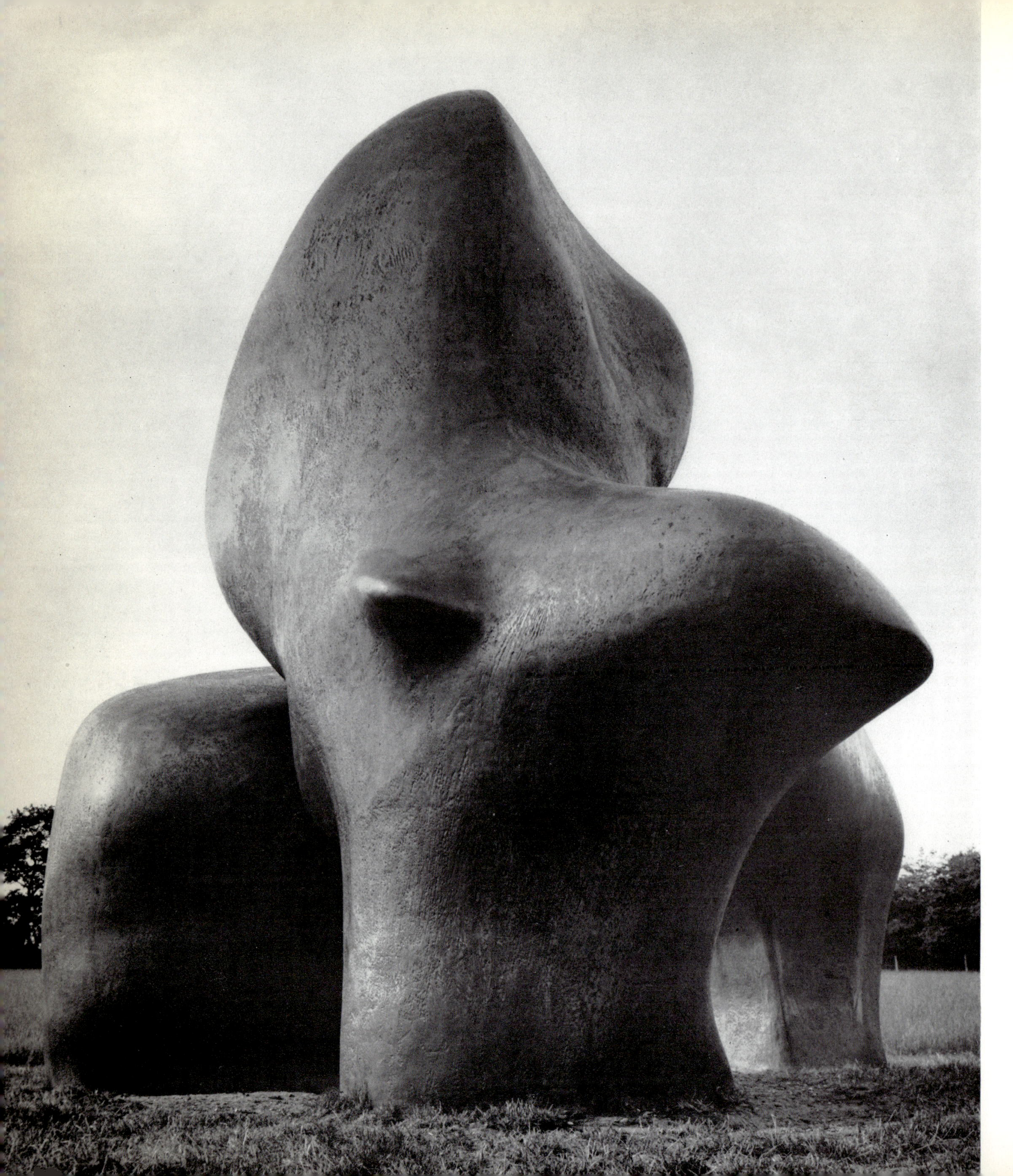

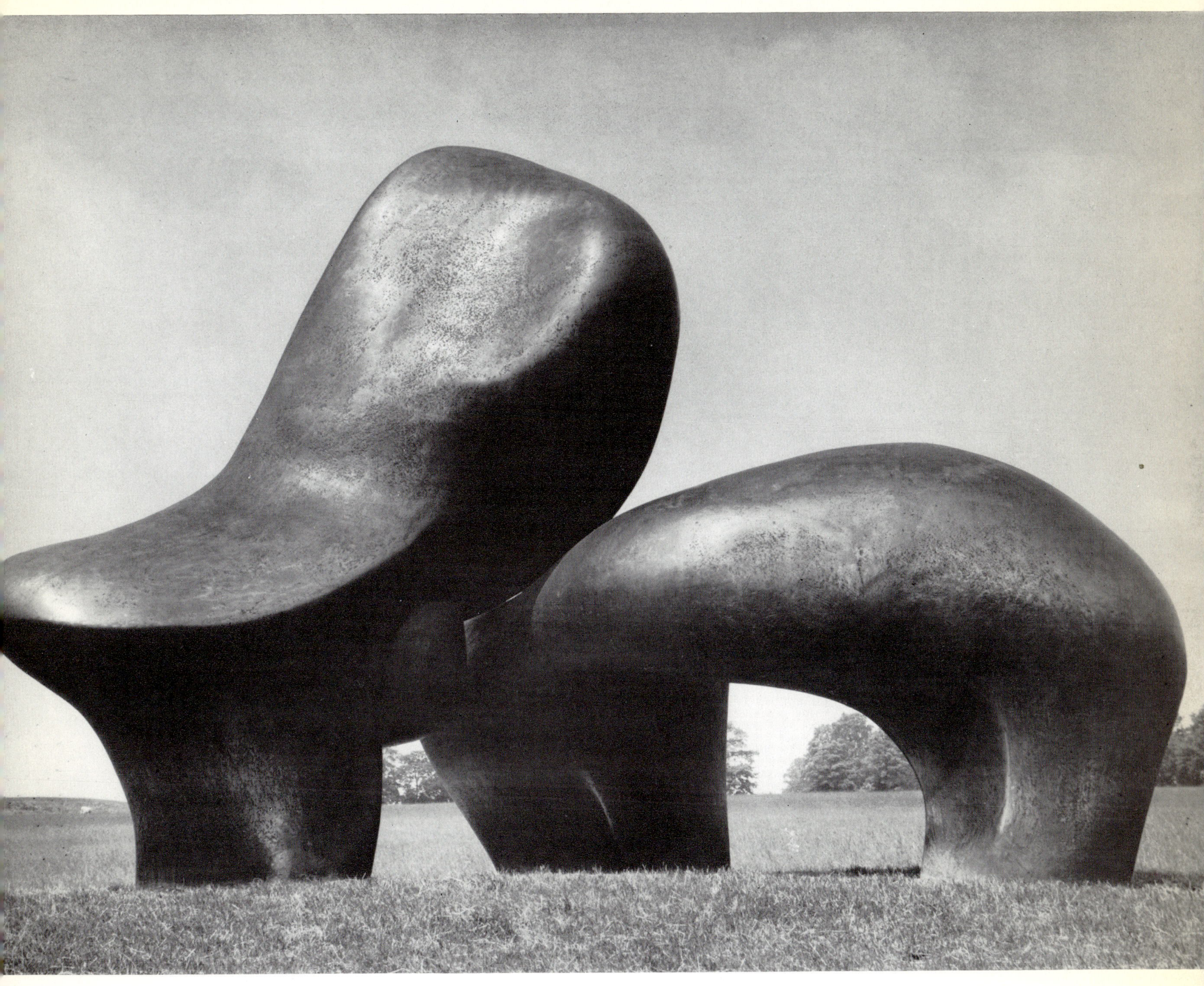

Plates 22, 23 **Sheep Piece** 1971–72 *length* 5.69m (12)

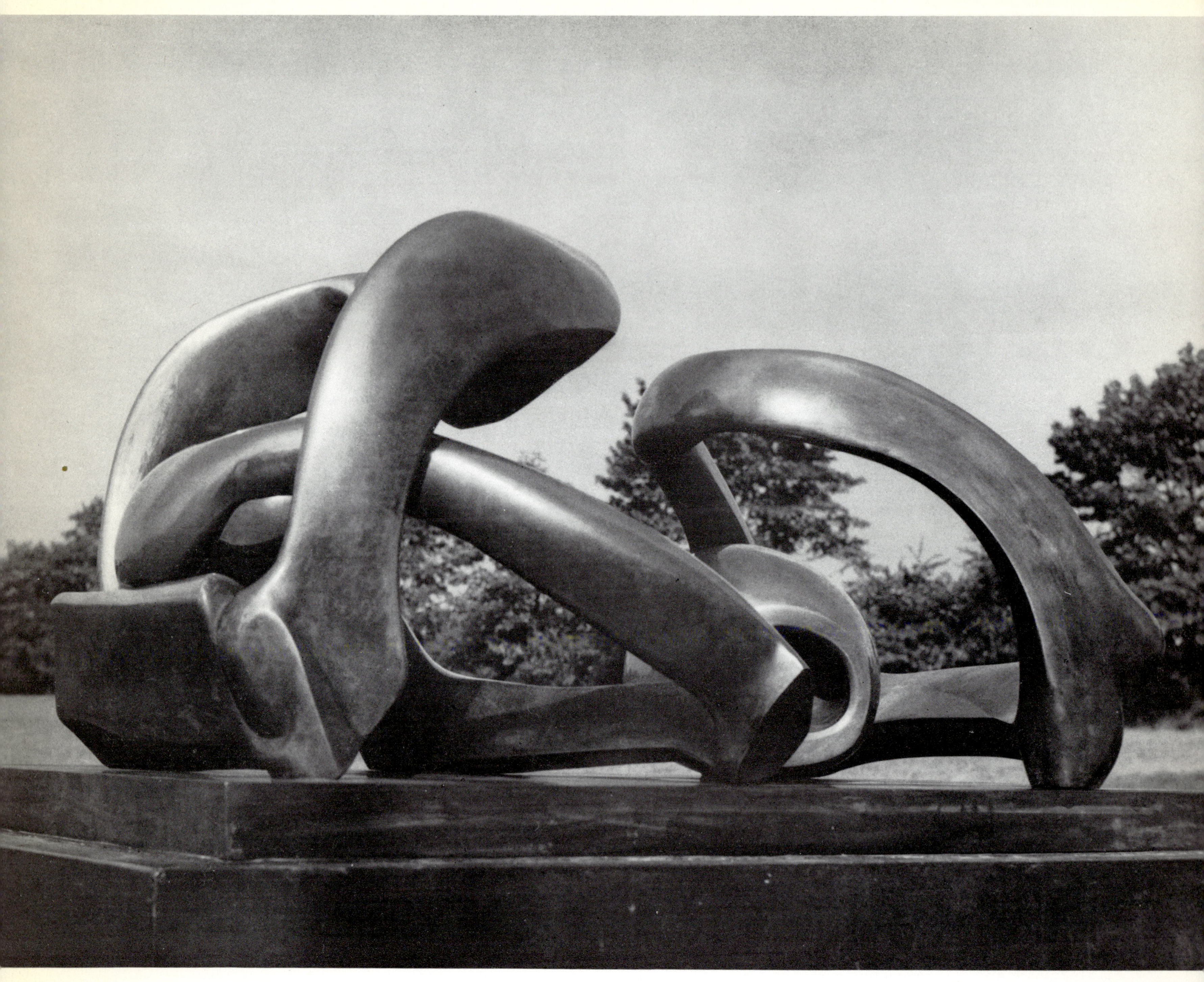

Plates 24, 25 **Working Model for Hill Arches** 1972 *length* 1.90m (13)

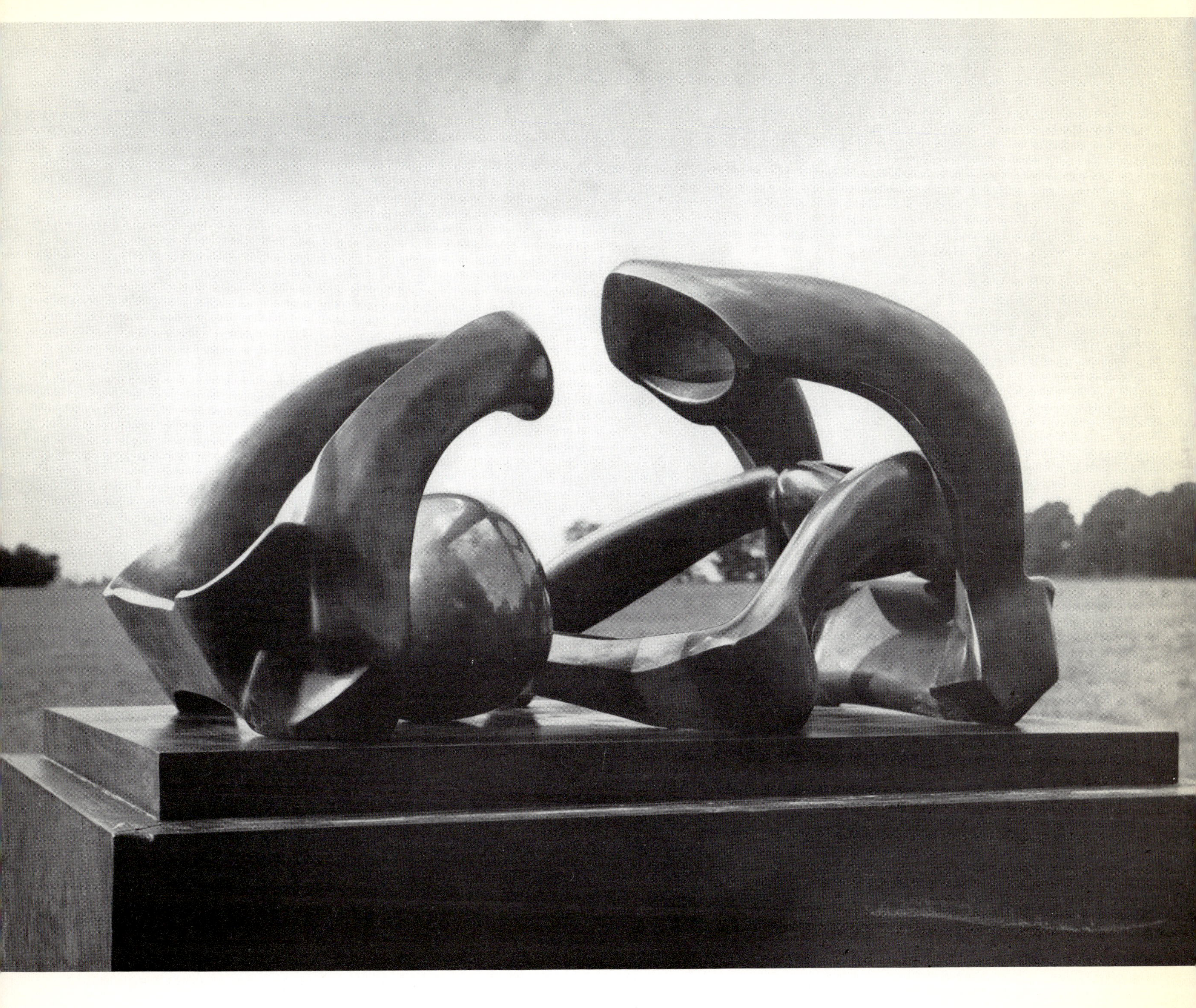

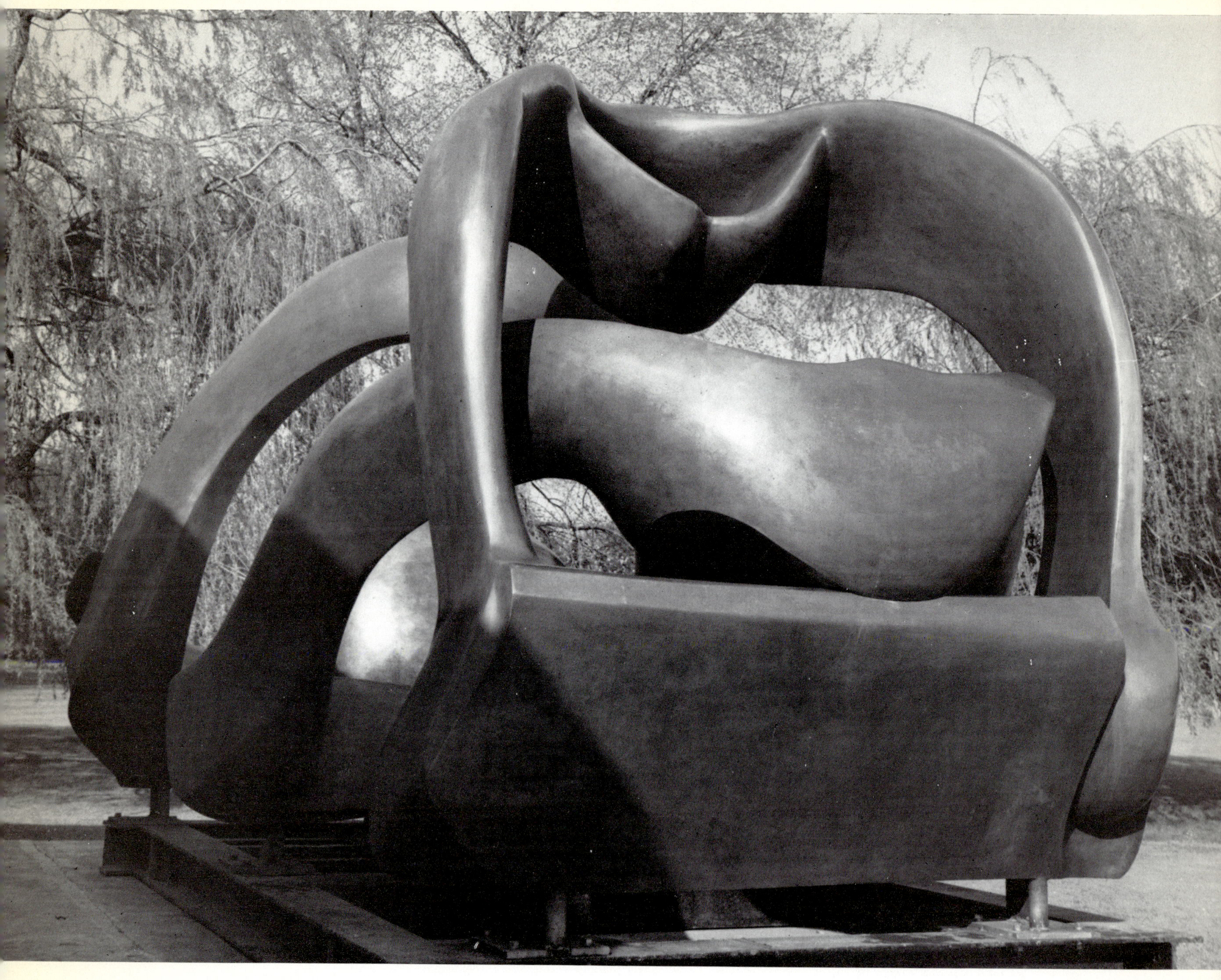

Plates 26, 27 **Hill Arches** 1973 *length* 3.96m (14)

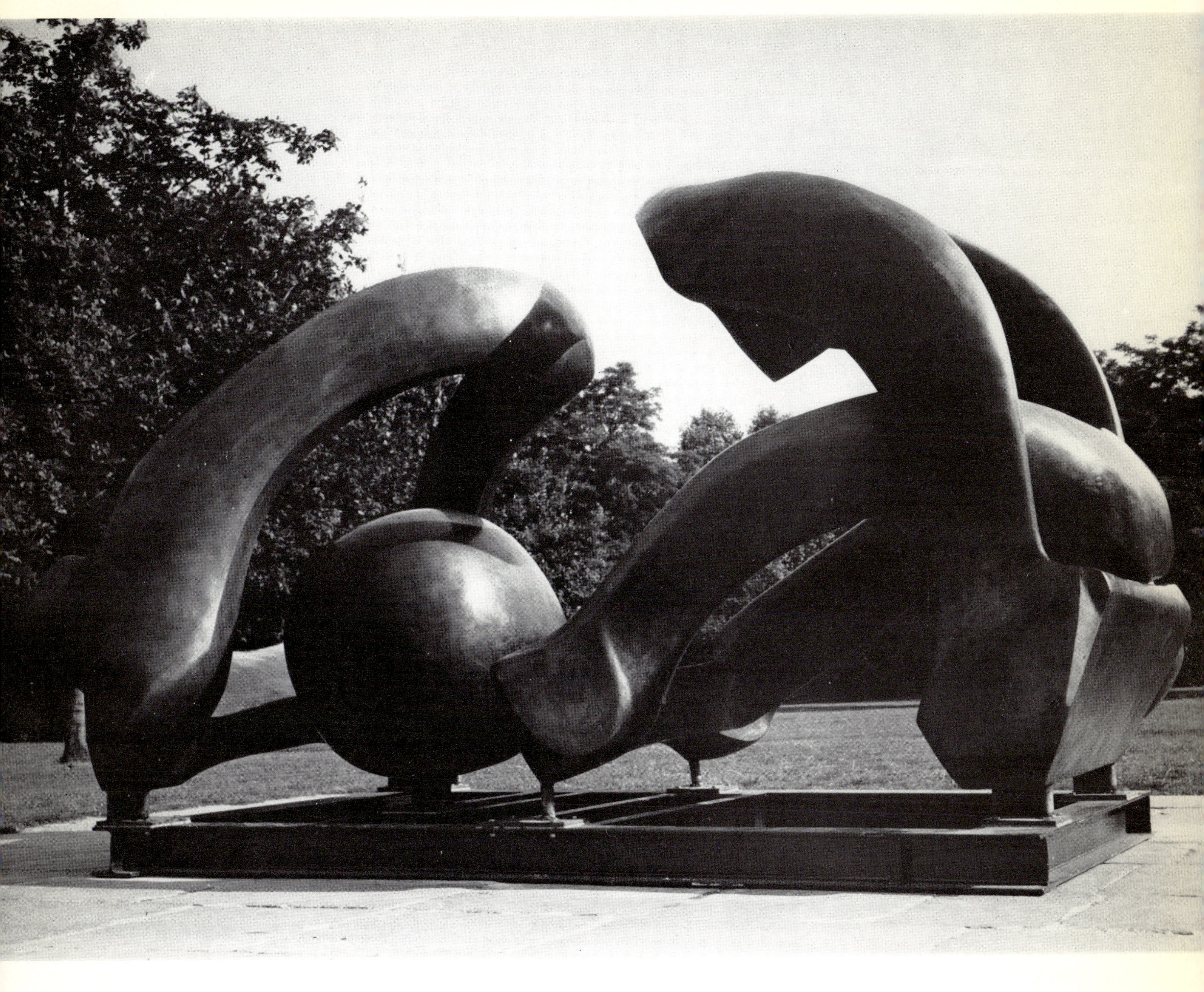

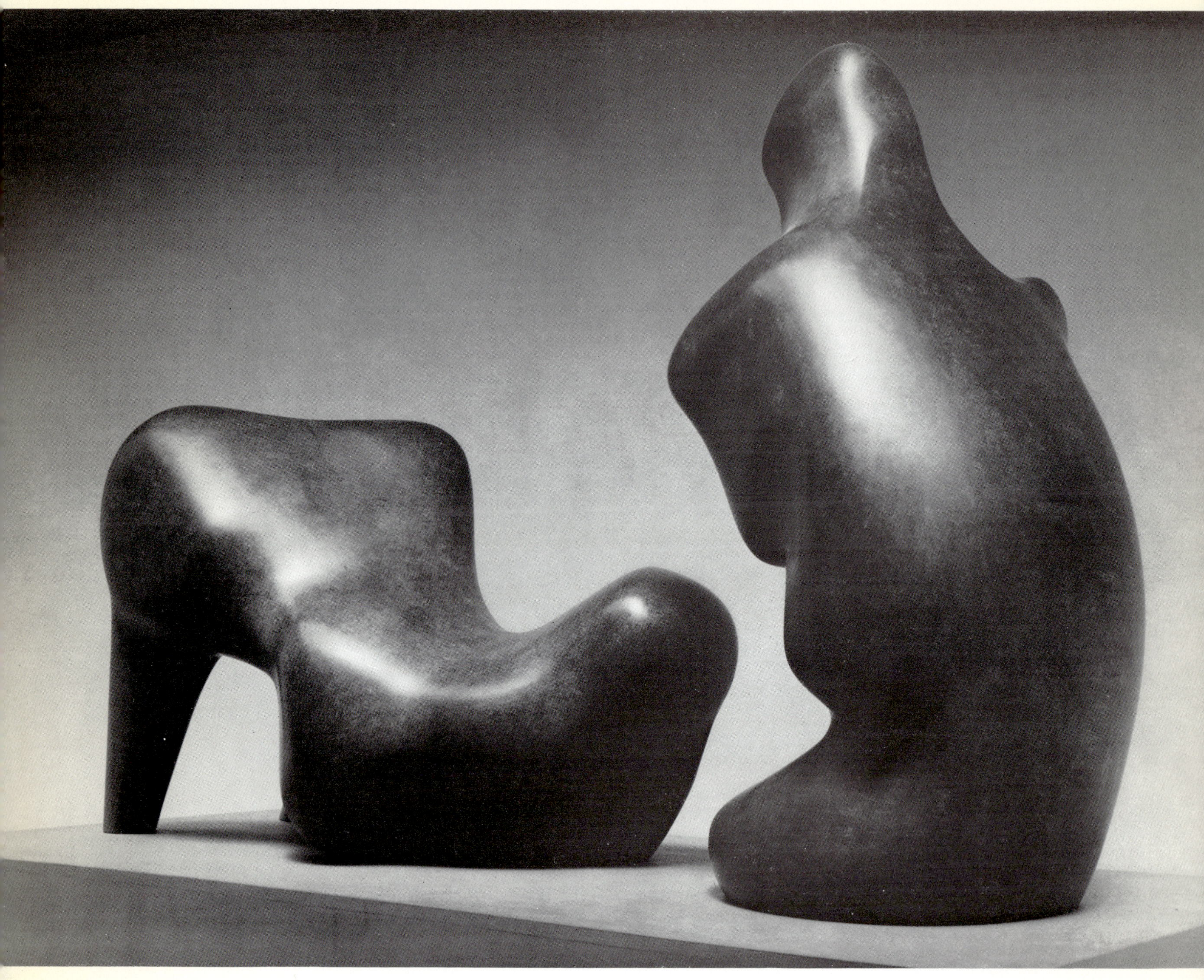

Plates 28, 29 **Two Piece Reclining Figure: Armless** 1977 *length* 2.22m (19)

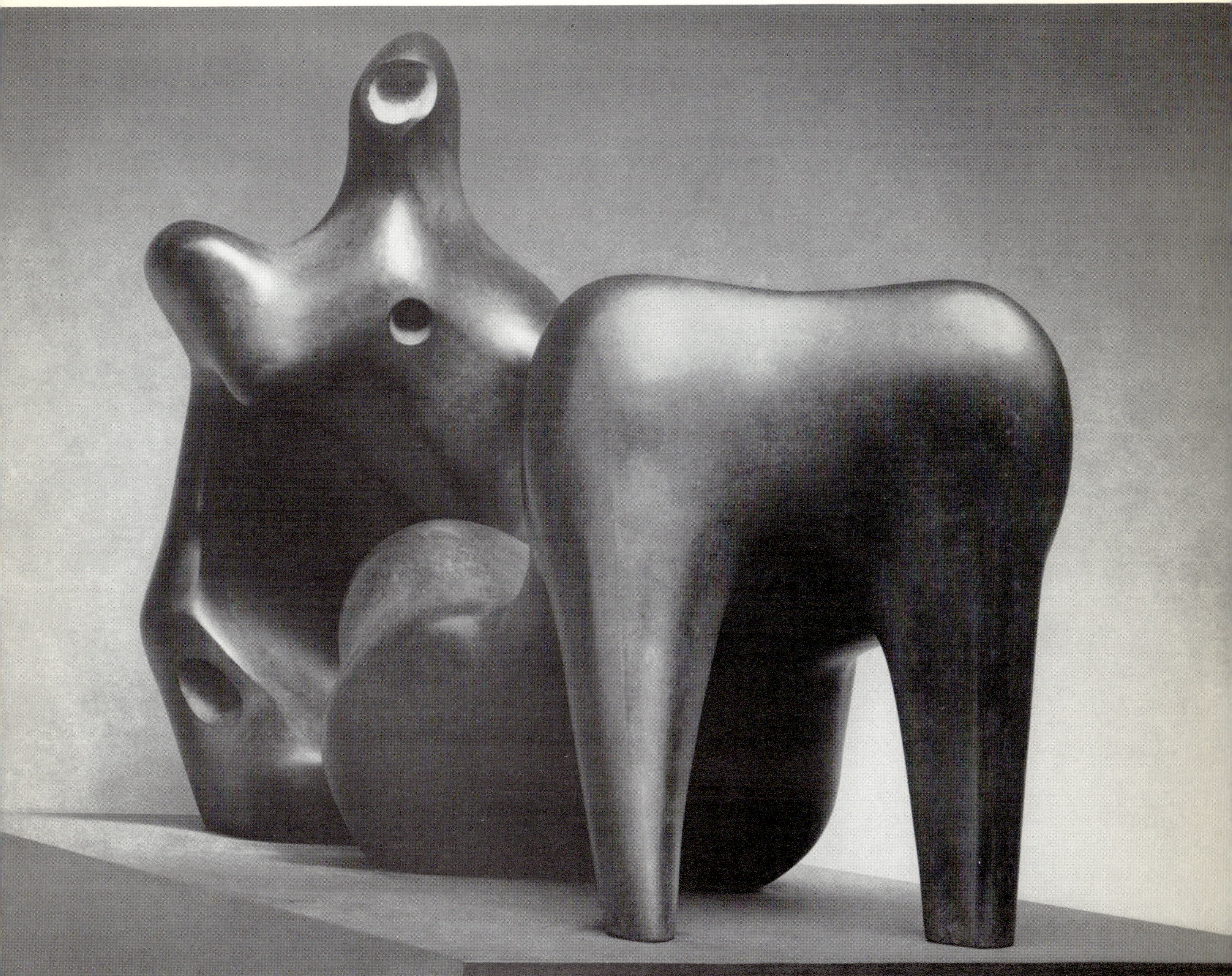

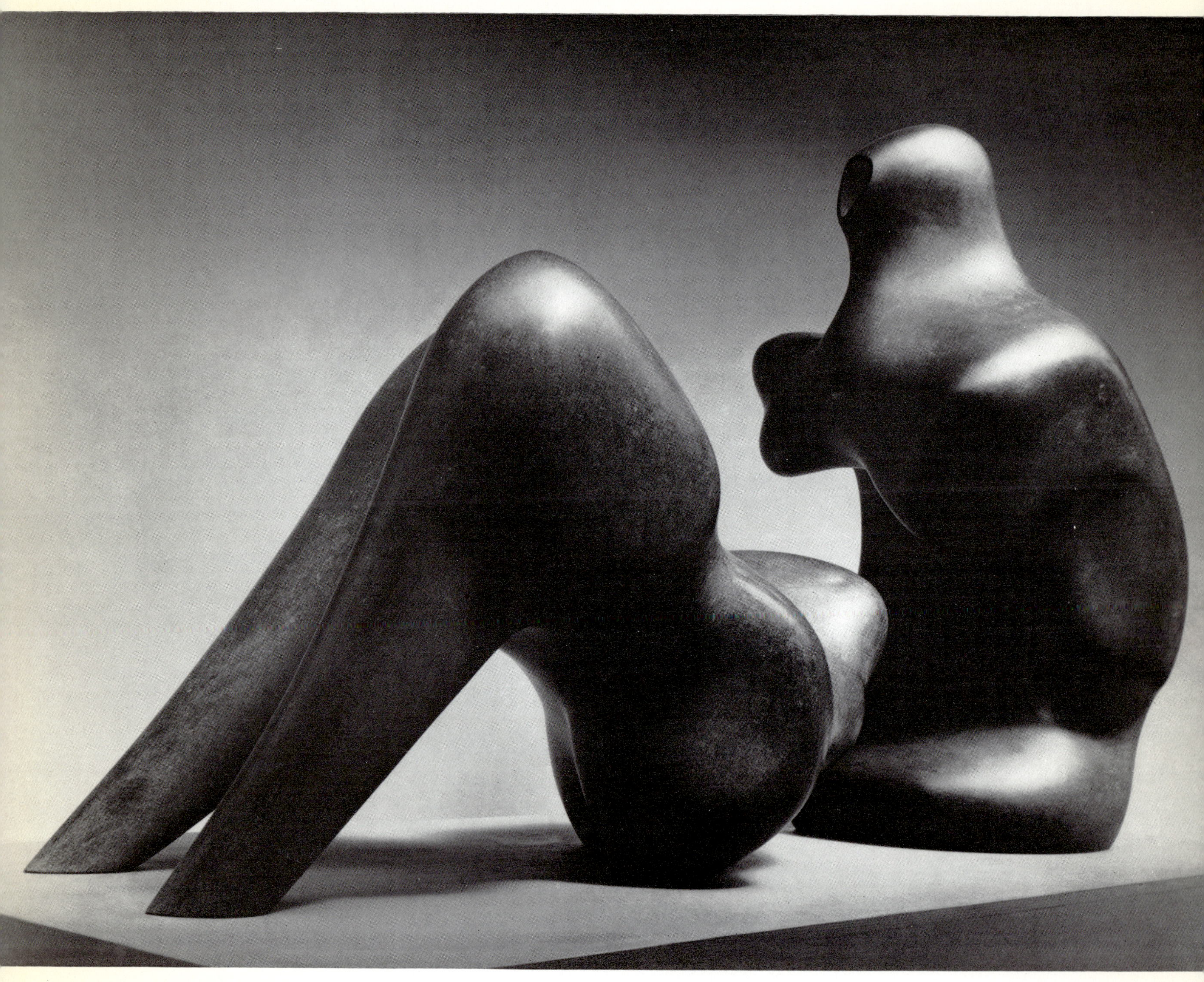

Plate 30 Two Piece Reclining Figure: Armless 1977 *length* 2.22m (19)

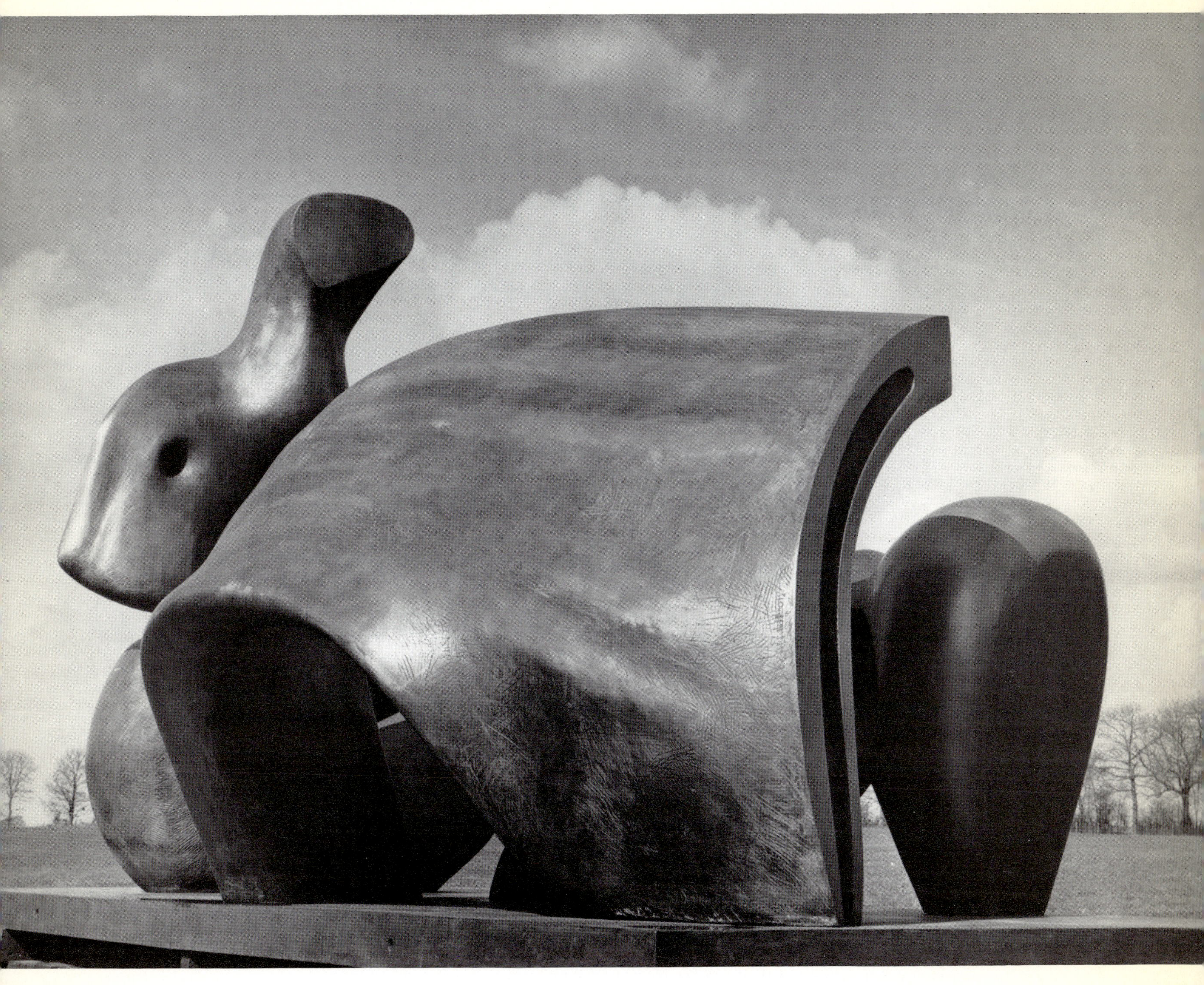

Plate 31 **Three Piece Reclining Figure: Draped** 1975 *length* 4.42m (16)

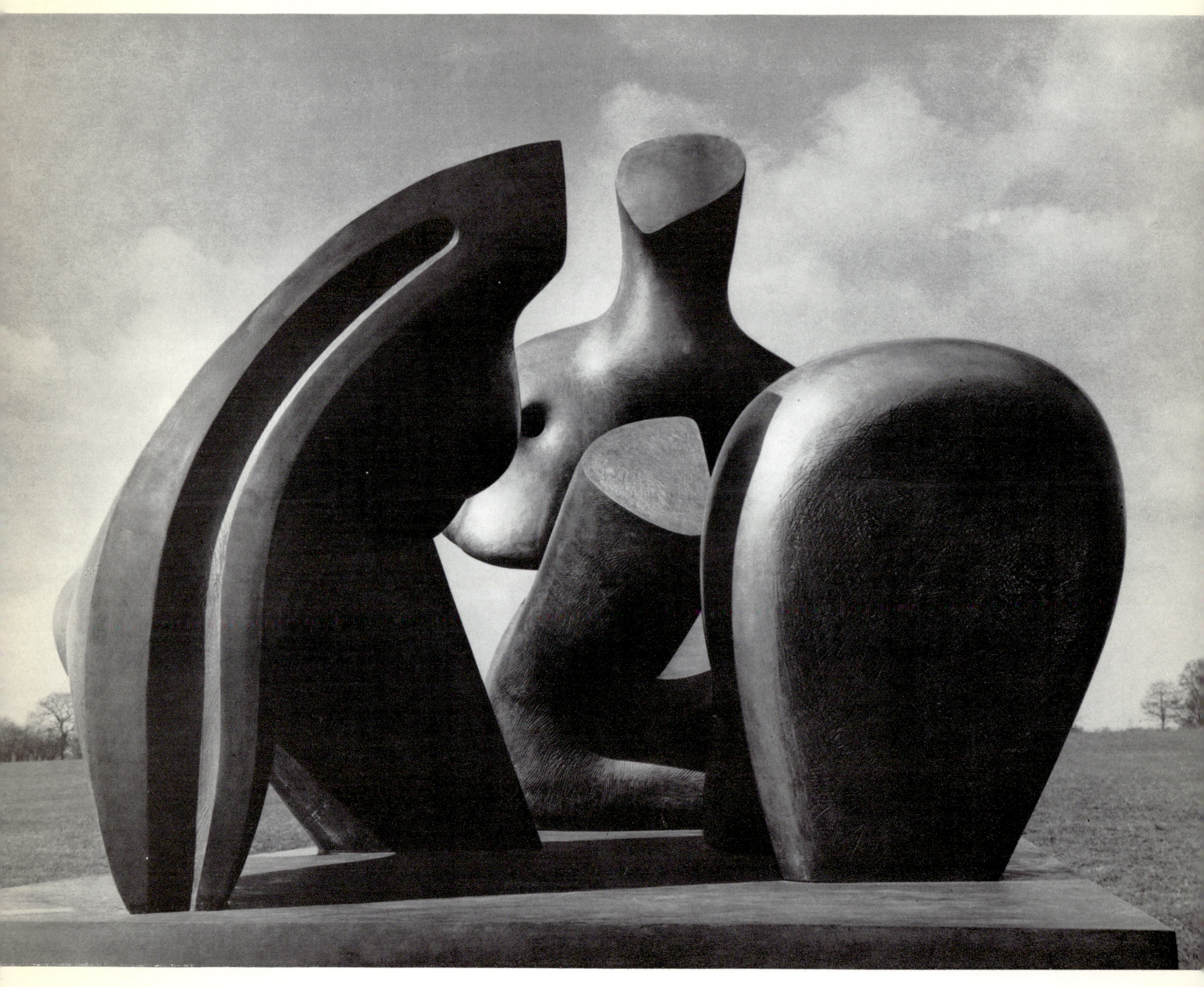

Plates 32, 33 **Three Piece Reclining Figure: Draped** 1975 *length* 4.42m (16)

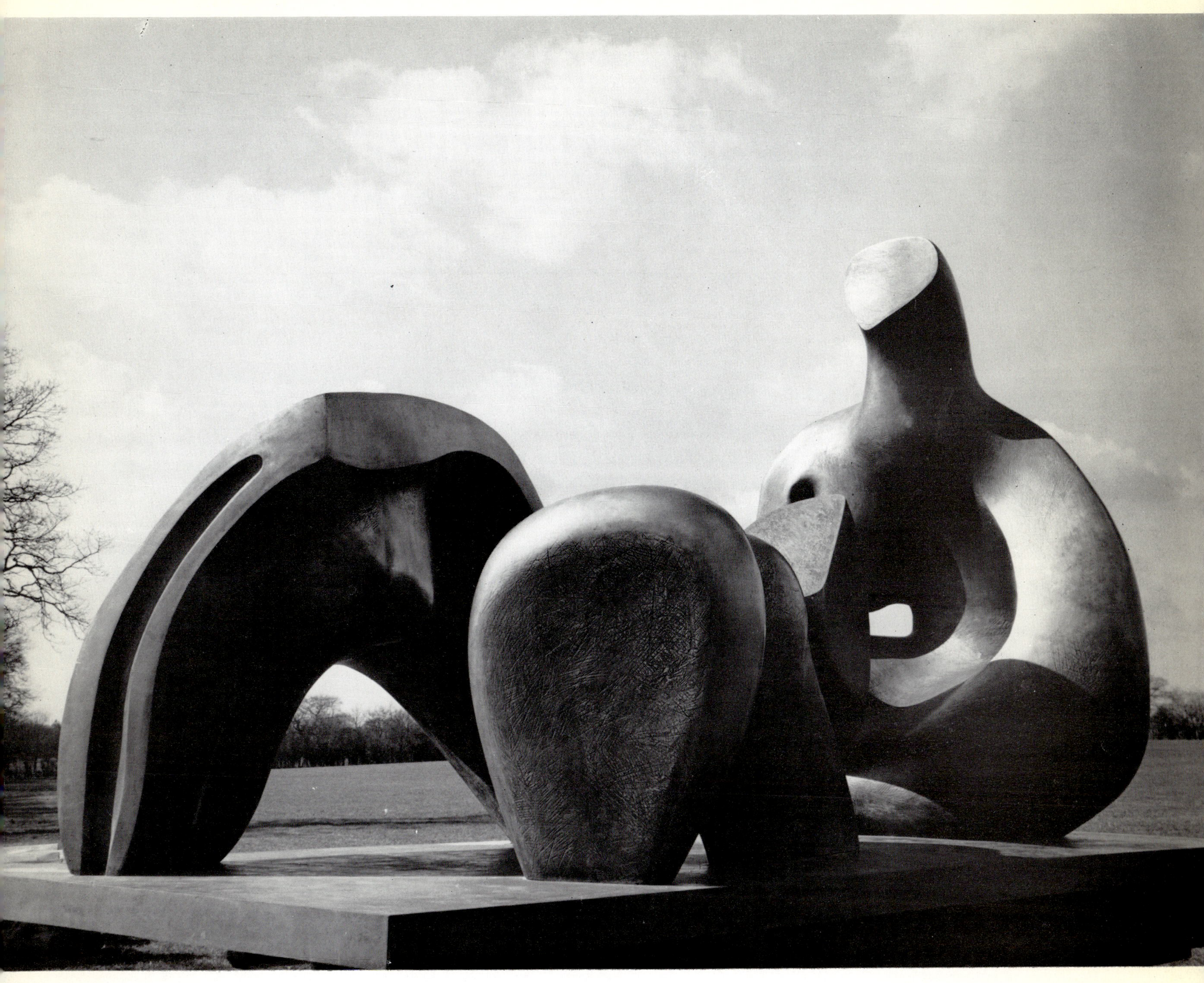

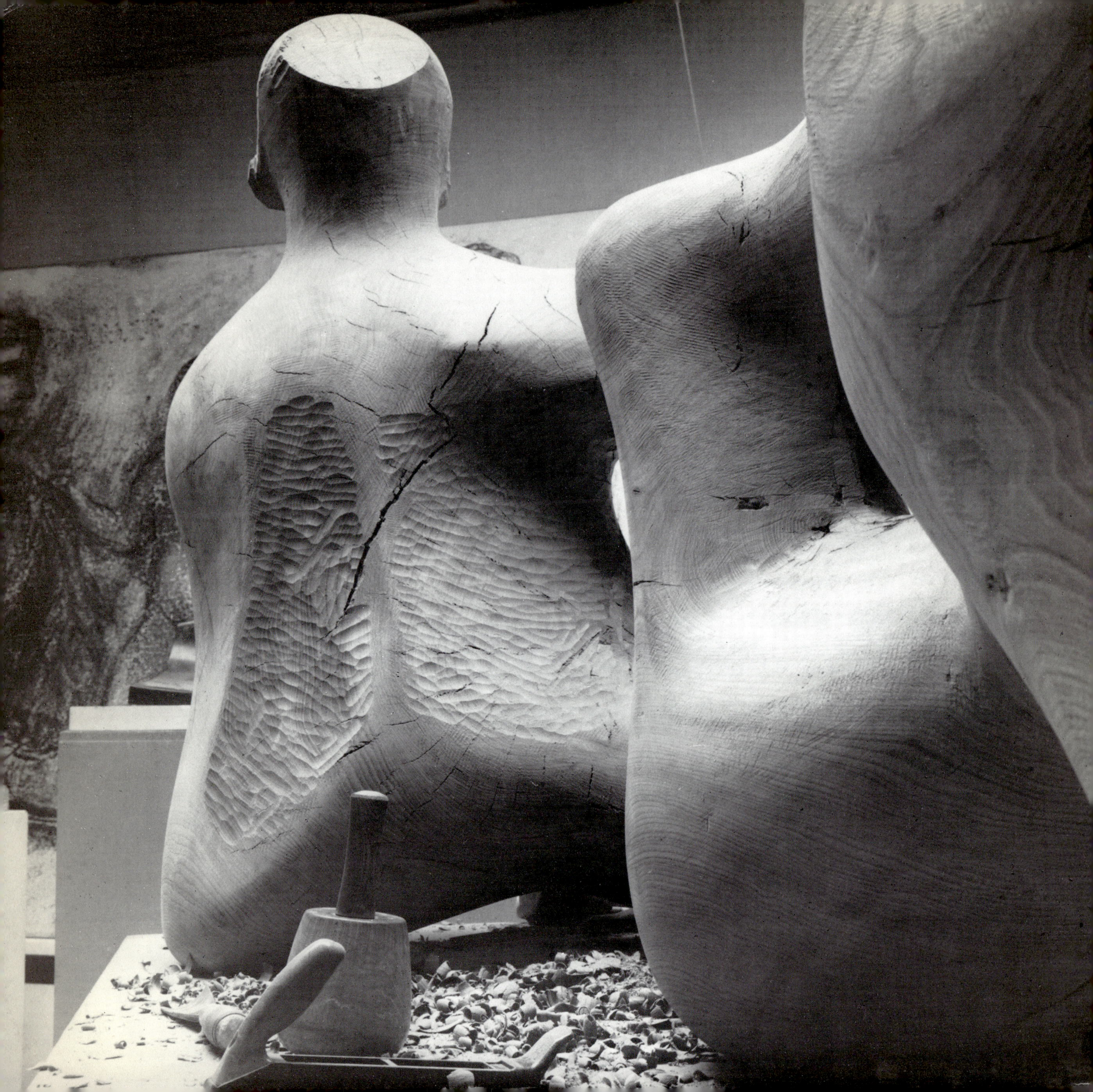

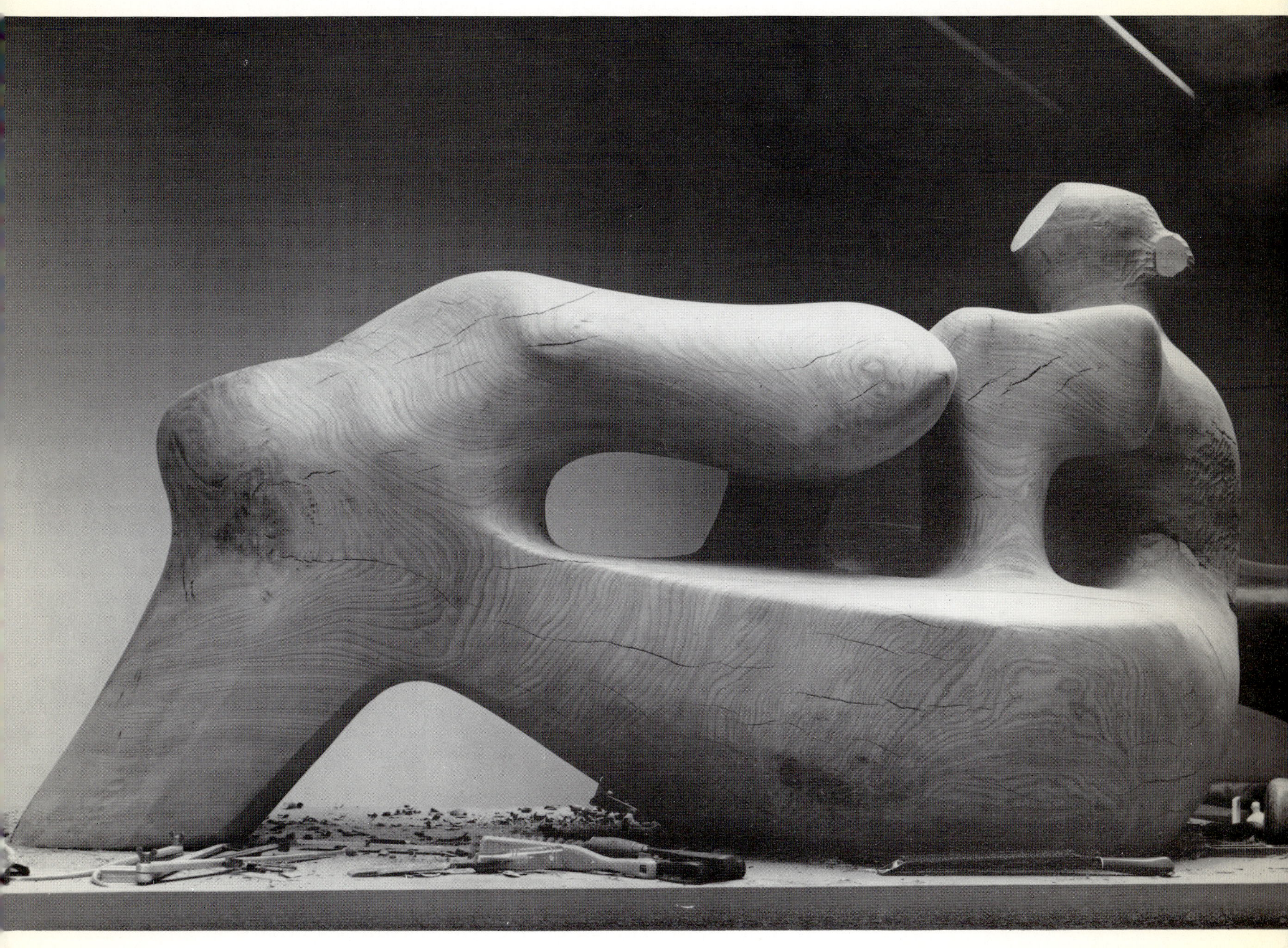

Plates 34, 35 **Reclining Figure: Holes** 1976–78 *length* 2.23m (18) in progress

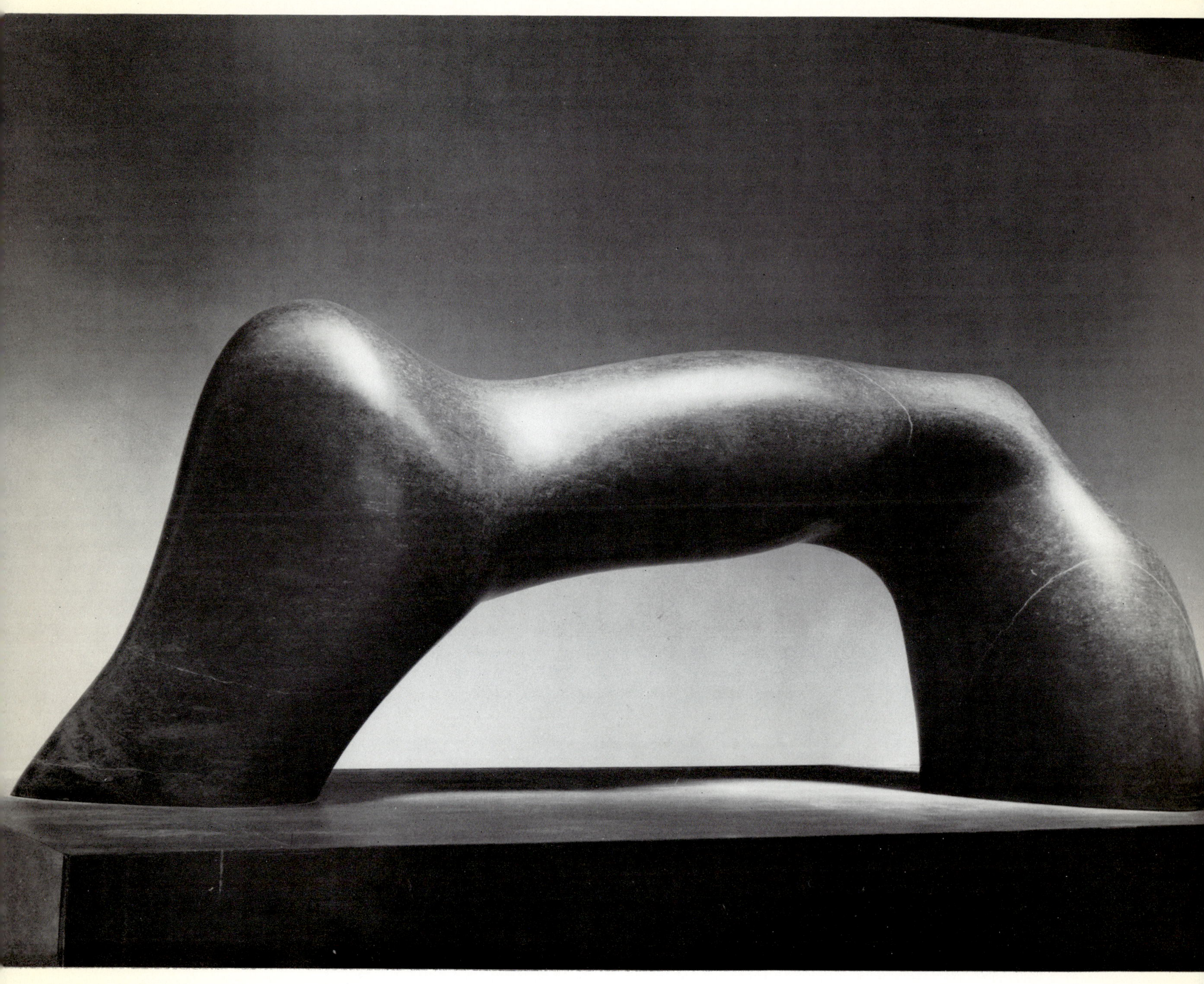

Plate 36 **Arch Form** 1970 *length* 2.13m (11)

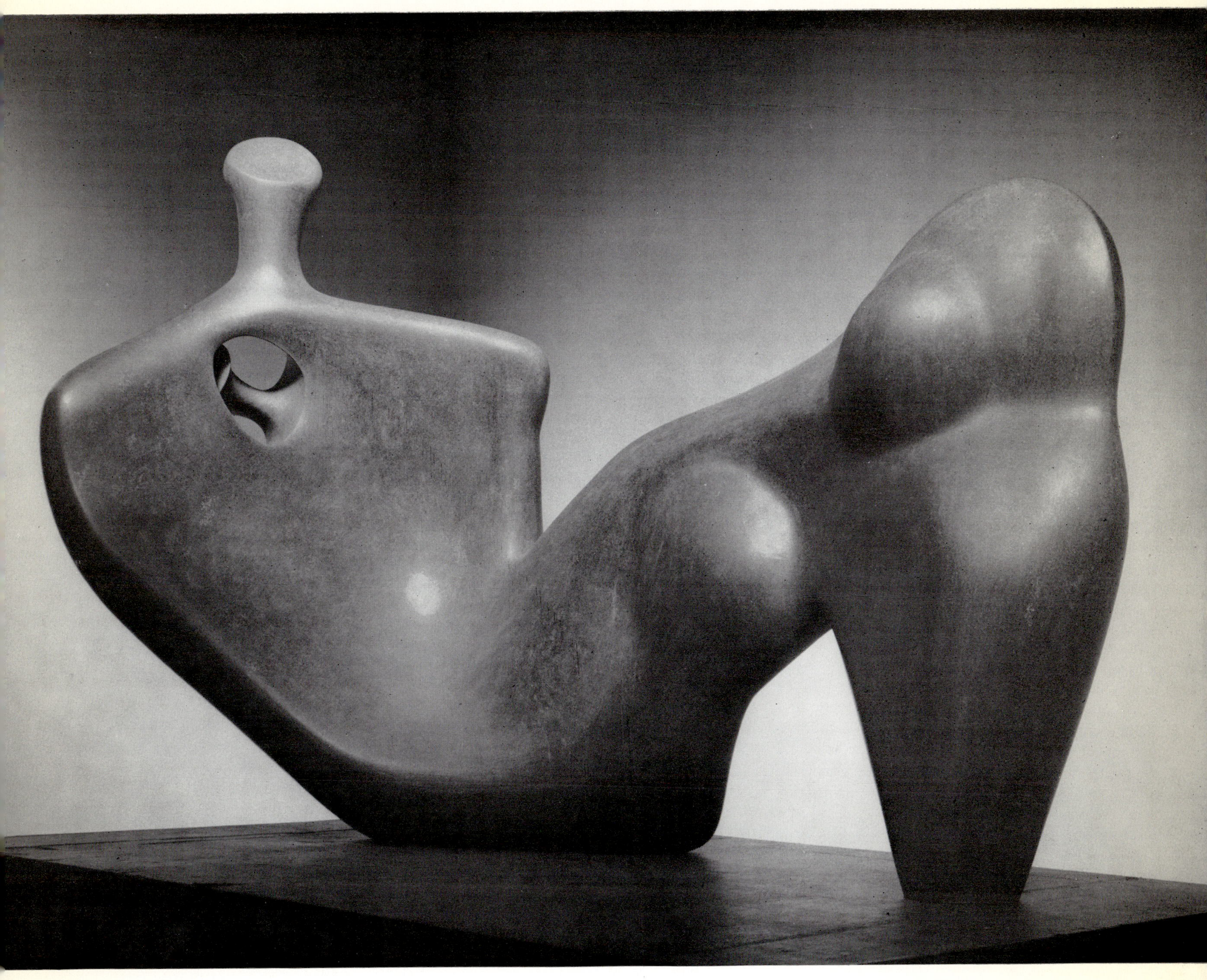

Plate 37 **Reclining Figure: Single Leg** 1976–77 *length* 1.85m (20)

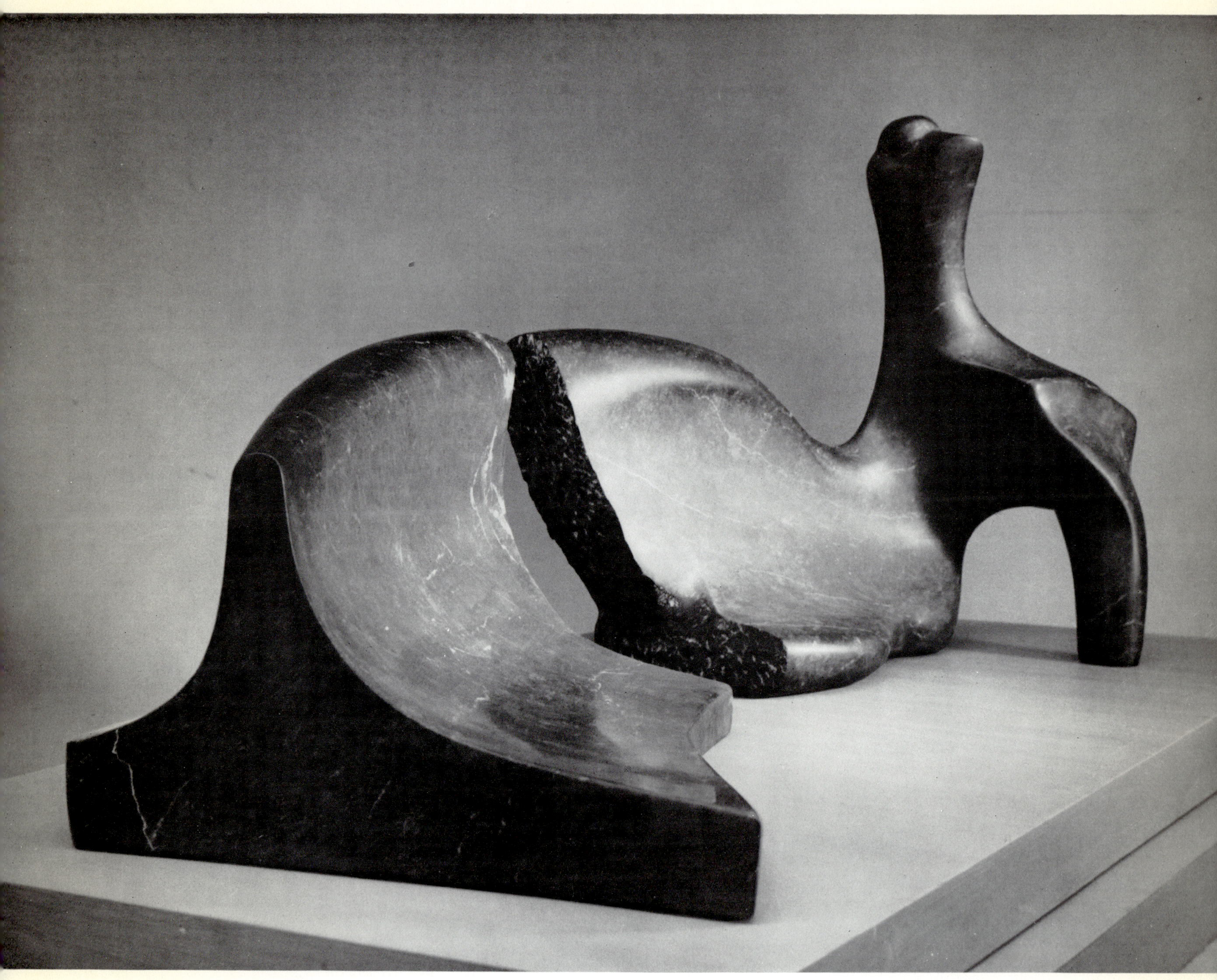

Plate 38 **Broken Figure** 1975 *length* 1.09m (17)

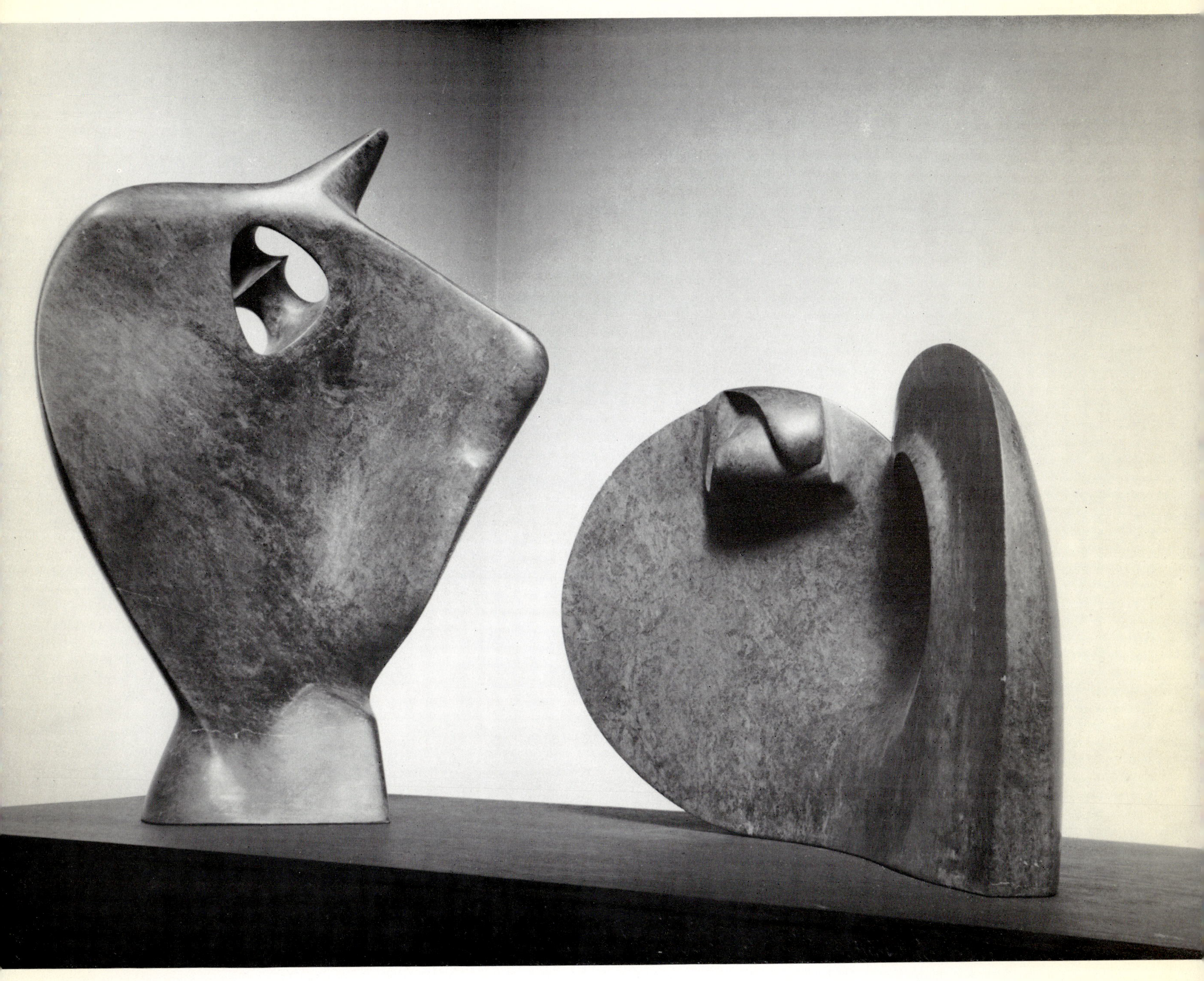

Plate 39 **Two Piece Reclining Figure: Double Circle** 1976 *length* 1.19m (21)

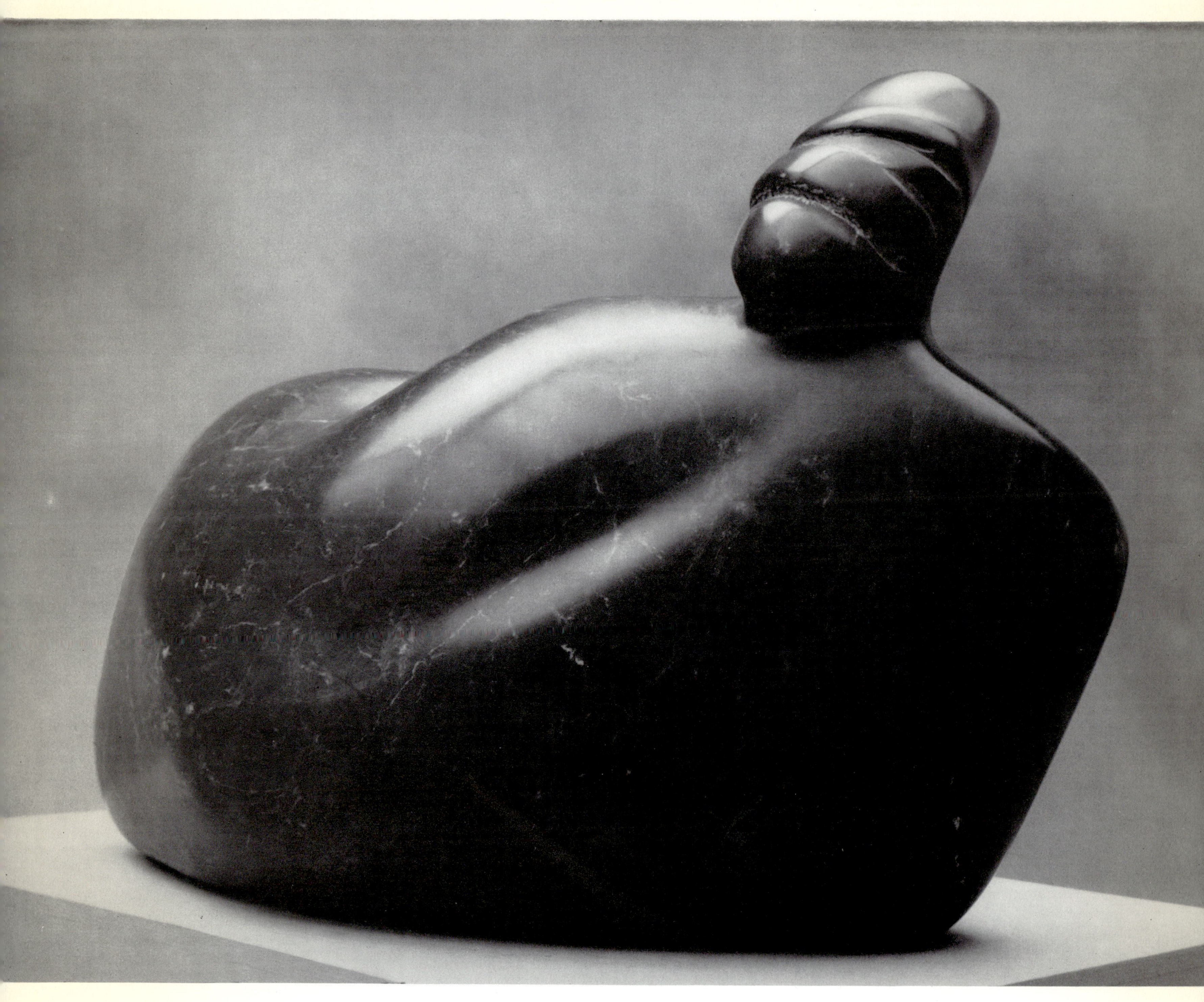

Plates 40, 41 **Reclining Figure: Curved** 1977 *length* 1.44m (22)

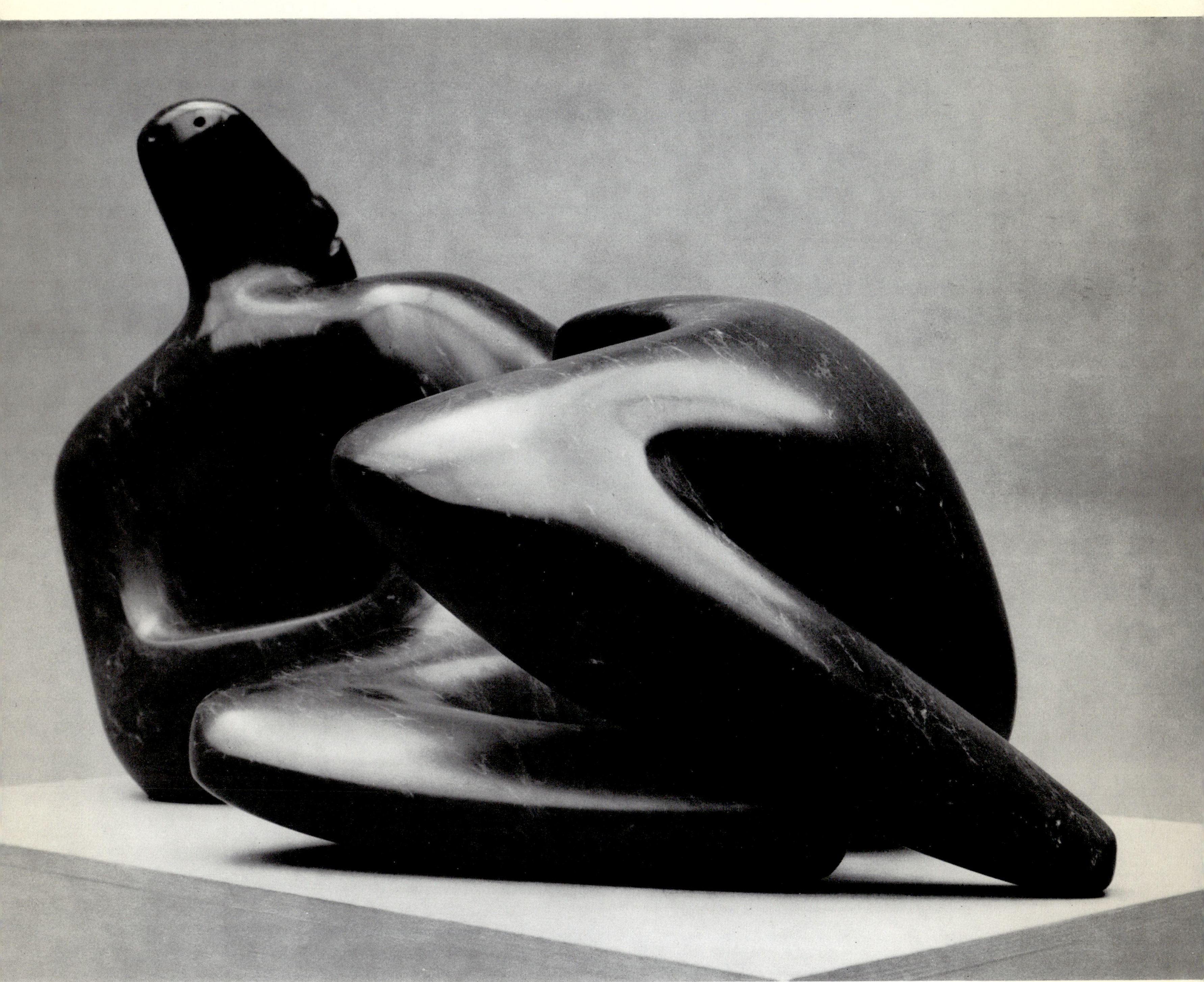

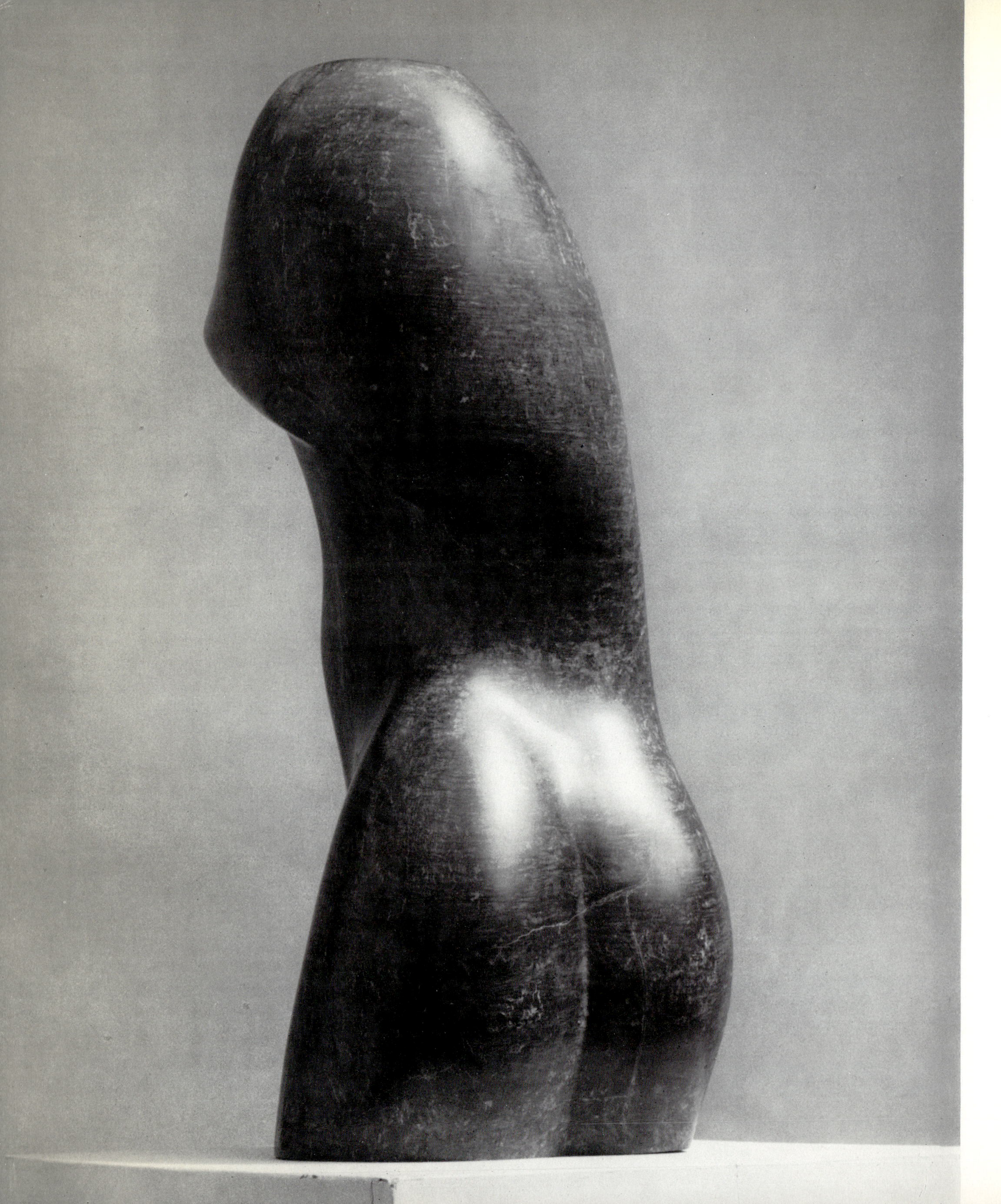

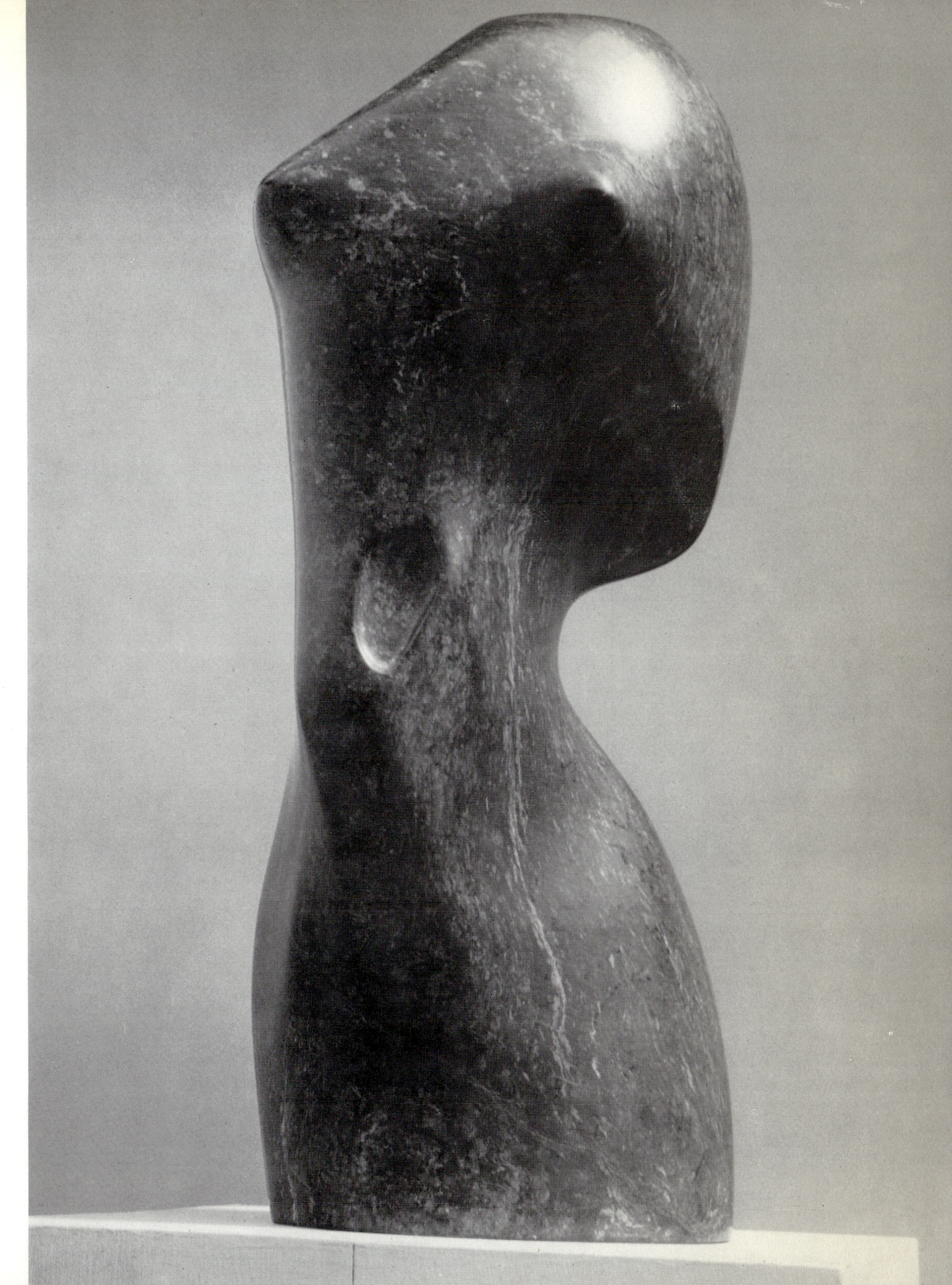

Plates 42, 43
Torso 1977
height 0.68m (24)

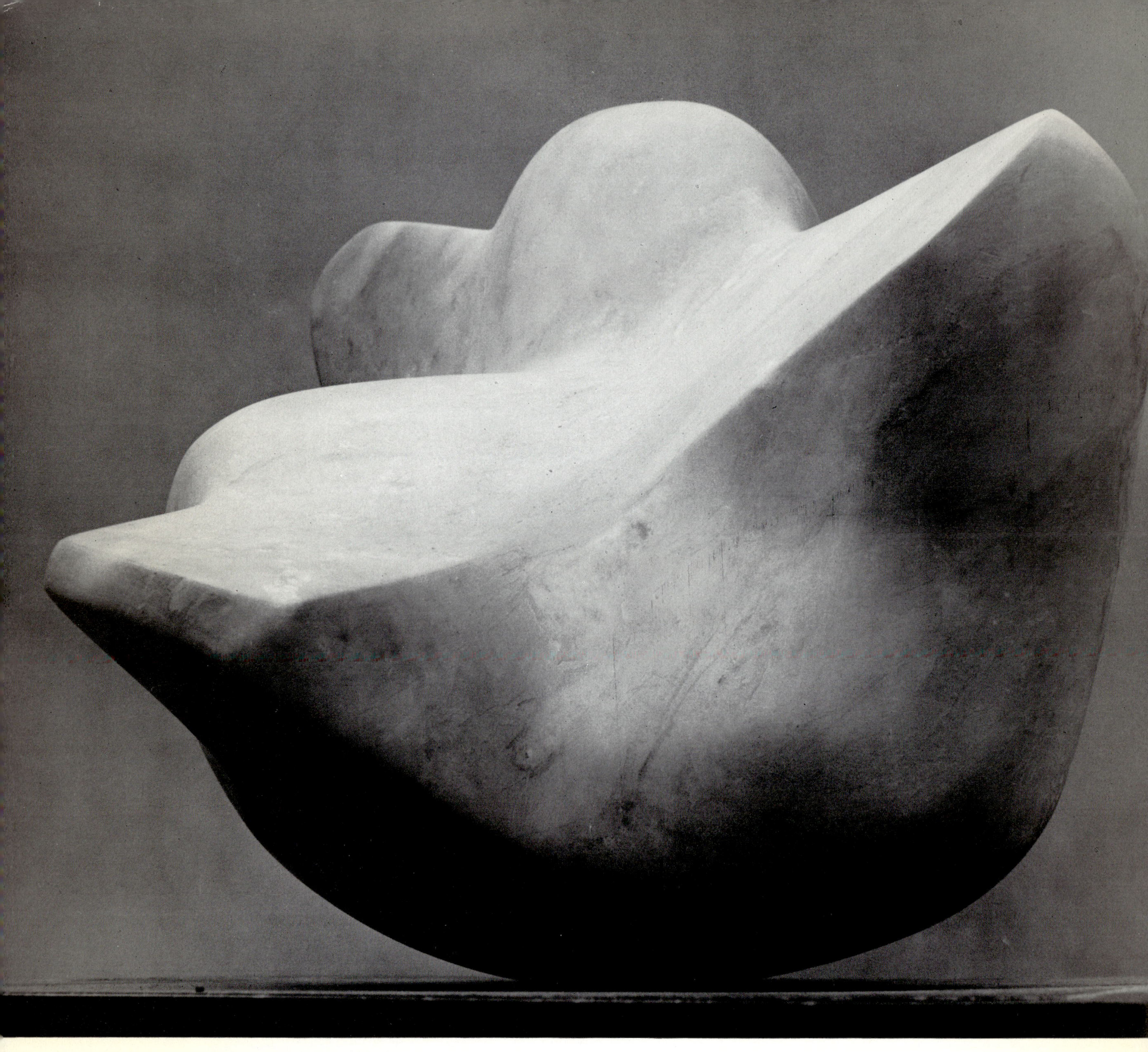

Plates 44, 45 **Butterfly** 1977 *length* 0.47m (23)

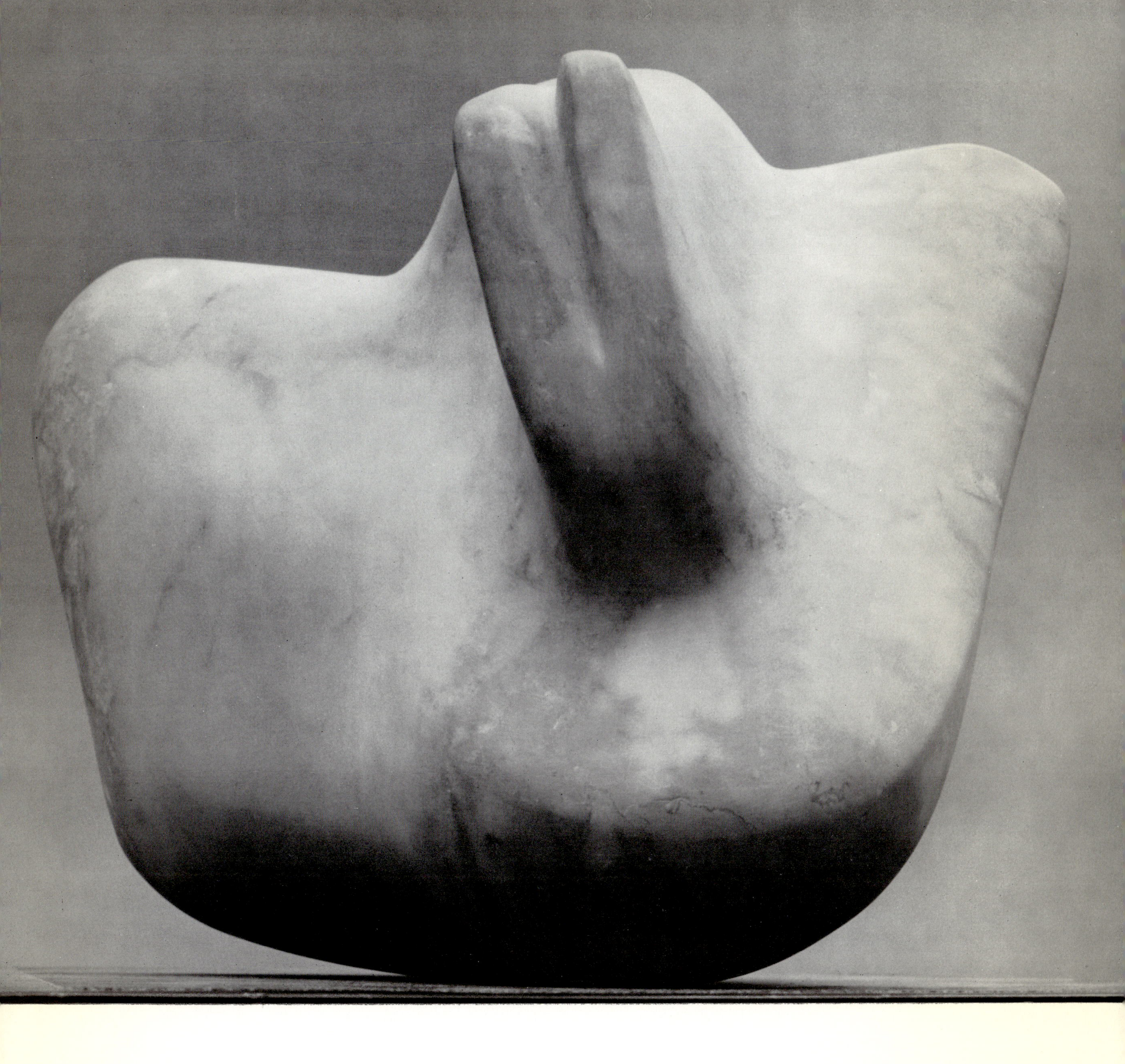

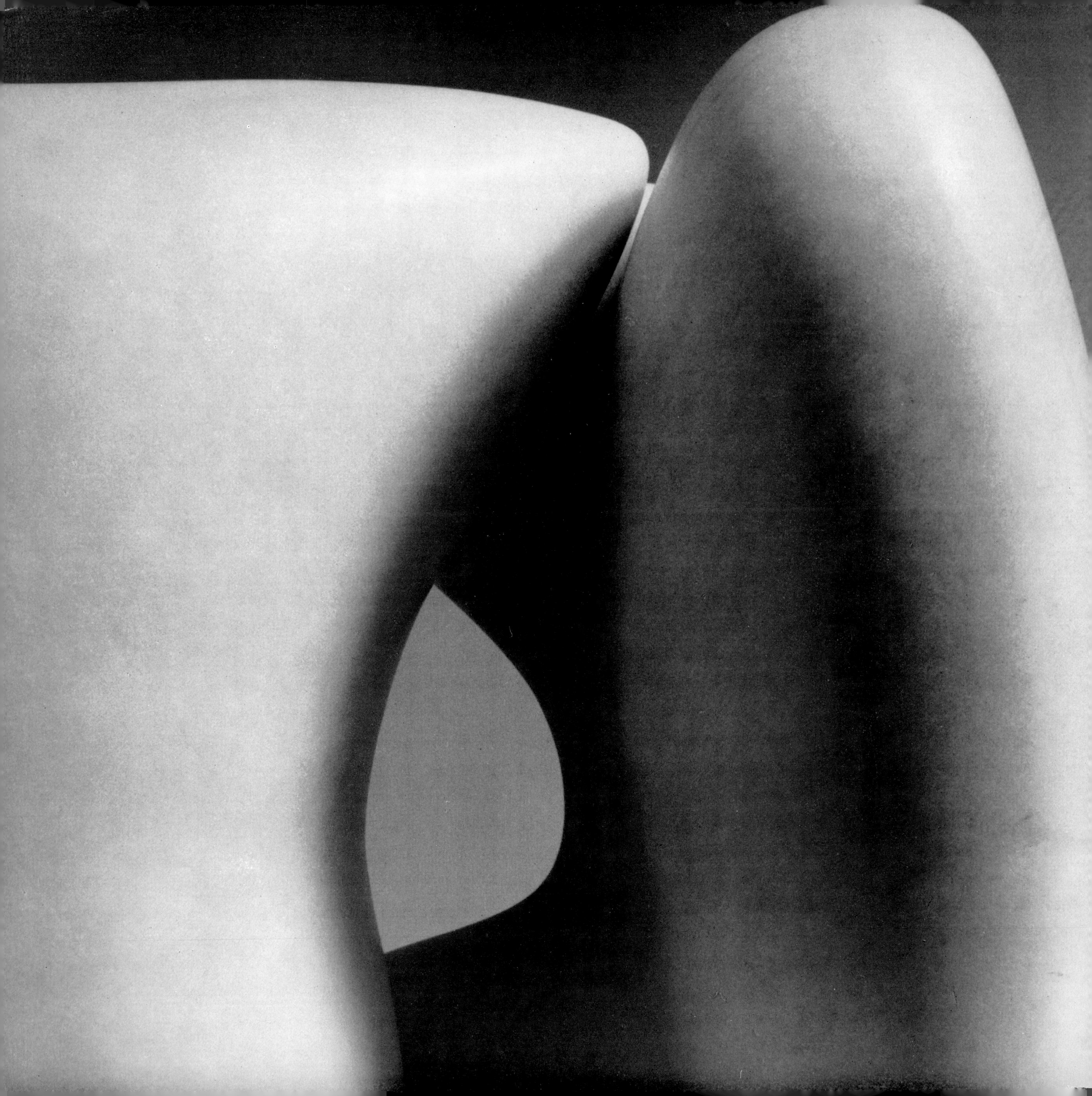

CATALOGUE

The works are listed in order of execution of the bronze maquette. The measurement of the greatest dimension is given in metres. The site numbers refer to those given on the plan on the inside back cover which indicates the sites of the open-air sculptures.

1 *Plates 2, 3*
Reclining Figure 1959–64
Elm wood *length* 2.28m
from a maquette
Reclining Figure No. 6 1954

2 *Plates 4, 5*
Reclining Mother and Child 1960–61
Bronze *length* 2.20m
Site no. 1

3 *Plate 7*
The Arch 1969
Fibreglass *height* 5.48m
from a maquette
Large Torso: Arch 1962
Site no. 9

4 *Plates 8, 9*
Large Two Forms 1969
Bronze *length* 6.11m
from a maquette
Two Forms 1966
Site no. 3

5 *Plates 10, 11, 46*
Mother and Child 1967
Rosa aurora marble *length* 1.30m

6 *Plates 12, 13*
Three Piece Sculpture: Vertebrae 1968–69
Bronze *length* 6.46m
from a maquette
Three Piece No. 3: Vertebrae 1968
Site no. 4

7 *Plates 14, 15*
Two Piece Carving: Interlocking 1968
White marble *length* 0.71m
from a maquette
Two Piece Sculpture No. 11 1968

8 *Plate 16*
Bust of Girl: Two Piece 1968
Rosa aurora marble *height* 0.78m

9 *Plates 18, 19*
Large Spindle Piece 1974
Bronze *height* 3.35m
from a maquette
Spindle Piece 1968
Site no. 5

10 *Plates 20, 21*
Two Piece Reclining Figure: Points 1969–70
Bronze *length* 3.66m
from a maquette
Two Piece Reclining Figure: Points 1969
Site no. 6

11 *Plate 36*
Arch Form 1970
Serpentine *length* 2.13m

Plate 46 **Mother and Child** 1967 *length* 1.30m (5) detail

12 *Plates 22, 23 and front cover*
Sheep Piece 1971–72
Bronze *length* 5.69m
from a maquette
Sheep Piece 1969
Site no. 8

13 *Plates 24, 25*
Working Model for Hill Arches 1972
Bronze *length* 1.90m
from a maquette
Hill Arches 1972

14 *Plates 26, 27*
Hill Arches 1973
Bronze *length* 3.96m
Site no. 7

15 *Plate 6*
Reclining Figure: Bone 1975
Travertine marble *length* 1.57m
from a maquette
Reclining Figure: Bone 1974

16 *Plates 31, 32, 33*
Three Piece Reclining Figure: Draped 1975
Bronze *length* 4.42m
from a maquette
Three Piece Reclining Figure: Draped 1975
Site no. 2

17 *Plate 38*
Broken Figure 1975
Black marble *length* 1.09m
from a maquette
Broken Figure 1975

18 *Plates 1, 34, 35*
Reclining Figure: Holes 1976–78
Elm wood *length* 2.23m
from a maquette
Reclining Figure: Holes 1975

19 *Plates 28, 29, 30*
Two Piece Reclining Figure: Armless 1977
Granite *length* 2.22m
from a plaster maquette
Two Piece Reclining Figure: Armless 1975

20 *Plate 37*
Reclining Figure: Single Leg 1976–77
Granite *length* 1.85m
from a maquette
Reclining Figure: Single Leg 1976

21 *Plate 39*
Two Piece Reclining Figure: Double Circle 1976
Black marble *length* 1.19m
from a maquette
Two Piece Reclining Figure: Double Circle 1976

22 *Plates 40, 41*
Reclining Figure: Curved 1977
Black marble *length* 1.44m
from a maquette
Reclining Figure: Curved Smooth 1976

23 *Plates 44, 45*
Butterfly 1977
Marble *length* 0.47m
from a maquette
Butterfly Form 1976

24 *Plates 42, 43*
Torso 1977
Marble *height* 0.68m